PRAISE FOR

How to Keep It Real

As a teacher, Drew Hall understands better than most, the difficulties teens, and young adults face in today's society. Few people understand how to instruct the next generation to "keep it real" better than Drew. In this book, he brilliantly relates the story of Peter's failure, restoration, and renewed resolve to show the next generation that they can move beyond mistakes, live for Jesus, and "keep it real" so that others can see Christ through them. Drew pulls no punches as he thoughtfully writes of the sticky subjects facing today's teens offering biblical principles to help them move forward with faithfulness and commitment in their walk with Christ. I recommend this book as a resource for parents, teachers, and youth pastors as they seek to help teens navigate this current cultural moment.

—**Kevin Blackwell, PhD**, DMin, Assistant to the President for Church Relations, *Ministry Training Institute*, Executive Director, Department of *Christian Ministry*

***

How To Keep It Real is the spiritual pulse check Gen Z and Gen Alpha need. America's youth is inundated with filtered falsehood of what is deemed "good." Hall's work brings this generation back to the question of "what does God say is good? And when God's goodness is not 'cool,' how do I walk in faith anyway?" While the presentation varies from generation to generation, this book will show the struggles of today's young believers do not differ from those who walked with Jesus himself, affirming that His grace is, in fact, sufficient. To those who might be leading young believers, let this book grow your curiosity for their questions. We just might have a nation of Jacobs on our hands who are bold enough to wrestle for a blessing.

—**Josh and Paige Wetzel**, authors of *Beautifully Broken: An Unlikely Journey of Faith*

How to Keep It Real

Real

Moving from Denial of Jesus to Radically Living for Him

Drew Alan Hall

Published by KHARIS PUBLISHING, an imprint of
KHARIS MEDIA LLC.

Copyright © 2025 Drew Alan Hall

ISBN-13: 978-1-63746-285-0
ISBN-10: 1-63746-285-9
Library of Congress Control Number: 2024950130

All KHARIS PUBLISHING products are available at special quantity discounts for bulk purchase for sales promotions, premiums, fund-raising, and educational needs. For details, contact:
Kharis Media LLC
Tel: 1-630-909-3405
support@kharispublishing.com
www.kharispublishing.com

Contents

Revelation 3:8: "I know your deeds. See, I have placed before you an open door that no one can shut. I know that you have little strength, yet you have kept my word and have not denied my name." (NIV)

Chapter 1

Class Dismissed

1st Corinthians 11:1-2 "1 Follow my example, as I follow the example of Christ. 2 I praise you for remembering me in everything and for holding to the traditions just as I passed them on to you (NIV)."

I grew up during one of the best periods in the history of the world. I grew up in the late 80s and raised in the 90s. Let me explain to you just how incredible this era was. We had Super Nintendo and the original Power Rangers. If you had a starter jacket from an NFL team, you would be styling and profiling walking into school, as WWE great Rick Flair would say. Time in school was also rewarding. If we read enough books and got enough accelerated reader points in elementary school, we would get a free personal pan pizza from Pizza Hut. I grew up when Pizza Hut was an actual restaurant. You could eat hot pizza right out of the oven, have unlimited soda refills, and play as much Galaga or Pac-Man as you wanted, as long as you could talk your parents into giving you quarters. Let me tell you, boys and girls, that we were royalty, living the American dream. They were the good old days.

We also had fantastic television shows during my childhood. On Nickelodeon, you could watch; Salute Your Shorts, Hey Dude, Legends of the Hidden Temple, Double Dare, and GUTS on their network. If you grew up during this time, you can't tell me you did not want to test yourself on at least one of those shows. Television also had real-life superheroes on it. Whether you were watching American Gladiators or professional wrestling, those guys and girls were larger than life. Hulkamania was running wild, Ghostbusters were who you would call, and Arnold told us to "get to the Choppa." It was a crazy time to be alive, but it was awesome!

Different characters from the shows during this time would pour into our lives each week. Clarissa explained it all to us. Danny Tanner was teaching everyone about life. Tim, the tool man Taylor, showed us that everything needs more power and could/should be modified. Steve Urkel showed us that it's okay to be a little nerdy. Television was also educational; Wishbone taught us literature, while Bill Nye taught us that science is cool. These examples only scratch the surface of the greatness of the 90s television. Yes, we were all saved by the bell, as well as being from West Philadelphia, born and raised. Friday was always a day of thanking God because you knew good shows were coming on the television.

If you were a child of the '90s, you were most likely influenced by one of the greatest television teachers of all time, Mr. Feeny from " Boy Meets World." Even at a young age, I remember realizing that teachers should care about their students the way Mr. Feeny cared for his. I remember the scene's impact at the show's end, where Mr. Feeny is alone in the classroom and says, "I love you all, class dismissed." The writers back then knew how to pluck your heartstrings.

Back then, I never thought I was going to be a teacher. But here I am 36 years old (at the time of writing this), teaching 7th grade. I am far from Mr. Feeny's status as a teacher, but I have created some traditions to show my students that I love them and to try to impact their lives. For example, before every test, I tell the kids, "Good luck, may the force be with you, may the odds be ever in your favor, and don't fail." I must credit my high school teacher, Coach Pierce; he always wishes us good luck, and may the force be with us. I just took it and made it my own. Another Coach Hall tradition is greeting the class with "hey kids happy and then adding the day of the week." For example, I welcome the kids on Tuesdays with "Happy Tuesday kids." At this point, you probably think this guy is weird, and you would be correct in your thought process. I tell kids every year that we are all weird; you just have to know how to own your weirdness. There is another sermon in that thought, but I will save that for another time.

Traditions

I started these traditions in my first year of teaching. I always wanted the kids to know that at least someone in their life loves them. I believe in my heart that words have power. I know this because when God created the universe, he spoke. All of the creation came from words. Words can give life and help build someone up or cause destruction and tear someone down. We have the opportunity to speak life into and over others. Sadly, the reality for some students worldwide is that words are never used to build them up.

Most kids will come from a home where they hear their parents or grandparents say they love them and are proud of them. I was lucky enough to grow up in a family like that. That's why I make it a point to speak life into and over my girls every day before we leave the house. However, there are students in classrooms worldwide who may never hear those words. Some students may never feel that love, affection, and encouragement from an adult. That's what a student told me during my first year as a teacher. The students had to write a letter to a favorite teacher who made an impact on them. The next day, I had a few letters on my desk. They all made my day, but one stood out from the rest.

Below is a copy of what the letter said from this student.

"Coach Hall,

I wanted to say thank you for making an impact on my life. For all the days when you asked how I was doing or simply said good morning. It gives me a little self-confidence. See, no one understands. I go home to a house, and they never ask me how school was or say I am proud of you for working a job. They never speak to me. You made a difference, and I appreciate it."

11

Talk about melting your heart. This one letter has stuck with me throughout my entire educational career. I had no clue what that student's home life was like. I don't know if I had ever even given it much thought. To be fair, she could have been having a bad day when she wrote it. When you deal with teenagers, you realize they can blow things out of proportion. Whatever the case, that letter has been a catalyst for me in my career. It's why I keep the traditions going year in and year out. Yes, they may be weird, but I never know the impact these little things might have on my students.

One of my most famous Coach Hall traditions is how I end every class. I took a piece of this tradition from Coach John Blackwell. He always told us to have a clean, safe, moral weekend at the end of each week. I took that and added the I love you to it. Everyone needs to overuse I love you. You may be the only person who tells someone those three important words that day. So, every Friday, my kids hear, "Have a clean, safe, moral weekend. I love y'all, and keep it real in the streets. Every day, when the bell rings, the last thing my kids hear from me tell them is I love y'all and keep it real in the streets (I told you I was weird).

The Process

It's cool to see how God works. After I wrote my first book (Tier One Christianity), people would ask me if I was ever going to write another book. I got the idea for the first book from something God used to show my family to trust him during a hard season of life. Initially, I thought it would be a sermon series I would preach to my youth on Wednesday nights. God had other plans, though. I enjoyed the journey of taking on a big project like a book. It was a process of working line by line and word by word. My wife always says that I am happiest when I have a project. She was right! It was my form of working things out. It was also cheaper than a therapist.

After going through the publishing process for that book, I started thinking of ideas for my second book. The first idea I had was different from this one. I could never make that idea work when I tried to outline the book. It just never felt right. Looking back, I was just trying to force it. Even though my heart was in the right place, the book could not work if God was not in it.

Then, one day, at the end of class, I went through the usual dismissal, and it hit me! I had been telling kids for years to "keep it real in the streets," but I never told them what that meant or how to do it. That day after class, I felt the same pull from God with this book as I did the last one. I knew I needed to add meaning and context to the silly phrases. My traditions are weird, but they all have a deeper purpose.

Each process of writing a book was a labor of love and filled with a consuming fire of purpose. I want to show you my mistakes for this project so you can learn from them. Please understand this is not a do-as-I-say, not-as-I-do approach to the issues we will discuss. This is a plea from my heart to avoid this behavior because I know from personal experience that nothing good comes from making these decisions. I know that either through pride, anger, or frustration, I have not always been the best example of Christ in my classroom. That is the one thing I wish I could change. Everyone makes mistakes, but I believe in my heart that heaven and hell are real. Every person with a pulse will go to one or the other for eternity. I hope I never turned anyone off from following Jesus. If I have, let me say I am sorry from the bottom of my heart.

My prayer and goal for this book is the same prayer and goal as my last one. I want to encourage and inspire you to dive deeper into your relationship with Jesus. I want to glorify God and share the gospel of Jesus on every page. I want to clearly show you that God, the creator of the universe, is madly in love with you. I pray that each of these truths will fill your heart with peace and joy. Above anything else, if you don't know Jesus as your Lord and Savior, I hope you are ready to take that step by the end of this book. The biggest question of our life is this: who is Jesus, and what did you do with him?

If you decide to take this journey with me (and I am so thankful you are), I want you to know a few things upfront. First, this will

13

require some self-reflection. Keep it Real in the Streets is not a project where we will be examining the actions of the world. We will look at some aspects of our culture. However, it is a project about you. More importantly, we will examine how you live for God and some reasons that could keep you from truly following Jesus. Please take some time to pray and reflect on your life and actions. To genuinely look at yourself and ask, am I truly living for Christ? That is a complex task for anyone, and if you are like me, it will hurt when you realize there were times you were not living for Jesus.

The second thing that I want you to know is that this is not a journey to shame you. It's the opposite. Will parts of this book be complex? YES! My goal is that no matter how messed up your life is, you will view and examine yourself through God's amazing grace. When you place your faith in Jesus and repent of your sins, God no longer sees them. Instead, he sees the sacrifice Jesus made on the cross. It was on that cross that our debt was paid in full by Jesus. If you believe that Jesus is the King of kings and the Lord of lords, it would be foolish to look at yourself differently than how he sees you. I want to show you how understanding this biblical truth can change how you approach God and respond to who he truly is.

Lastly, I want you to know that failure is only final if you make failure fatal. Too often, we mess up and then throw in the towel. Think back to a time in your life when you tried to start a new habit or healthy diet. We start well, but then we have a cheat day that becomes a cheat week. Or we get busy and don't have time to practice our healthy habits, so we skip a day, which turns into a missed week. I believe many people struggle with this same thing regarding God. We know we need more of him and to spend time with him daily. Or we know we need to avoid specific actions (sins). When we fall, we quickly wave the white flag and return to the old way of life. This approach does not lead us to where God wants us to be. Or to be the person God made us to be.

So now that you know what you are in store for, I hope and pray you will enjoy this journey. Some things will take hard self-reflection. During this time, remember shame and regret are not our target destinations. We always want to land on God's love, grace, and forgiveness. Remember, you are never too far gone from God. Failure is only fatal if you willingly stay there.

Chapter 2

Masquerade

Revelation 3:1-2 "To the angel[a] of the church in Sardis write: These are the words of him who holds the seven spirits[b] of God and the seven stars. I know your deeds; you have a reputation of being alive, but you are dead. 2 Wake up! Strengthen what remains and is about to die, for I have found your deeds unfinished in the sight of my God (NIV)."

Addressing the Problem

Kids are great judges of character. I know this is especially true in teenagers or pre-teens. They can see through fake words or actions very quickly. Adults can do the same thing, but typically, kids are less jaded than adults. When we pretend to be a certain way, but our heart is the opposite, we can quickly drive people away. Nobody likes to be around fake people. So why would people put on a show instead of showing who they really are? We are scared to show people who we really are. We know we will get certain things if we act in specific ways. So, the heart of our actions is purely for our gain. If we are living for ourselves, then that is completely fine. If people see through our acts and know we are fake, then the only person it hurts is us. When we take on the title of son or daughter of God, our actions carry more weight and impact more people than ourselves.

These actions of putting on a show are the very problem I want to address in this book. The example for this did not come from observing other people but from looking back at my life and actions. I realized there were times when I proclaimed myself a follower of Jesus, but my actions did not support that statement. A critical event sparked this, which I will discuss in the next chapter. If you are like me, you can find more than you did in your past.

The word Christian comes from the Greek word *"Christianos."* That word is the combination of two words. The first word, Christ in Greek, means "anointed one," and the second is *"tian,"* which means little. So, by putting these two words together, you get a little anointed or Christian. In our vernacular today, Christian means follower of Jesus. That description is precisely what our lives should look like.

When the world sees us, it should see little versions of Jesus. As a kid, you dressed up and acted like your heroes. I remember having a Ghostbusters outfit that I wore all the time. I see this with my kids today when they dress up as princesses. As a teenager or adult, is there a better person to emulate than Jesus? For someone to say, "We look like Jesus," should be the compliment we are all working for.

That's a great idea on paper, and it should be what we strive for, but in the real world, it can be challenging. If we are honest, we can treat Jesus like a Halloween costume. When it's time to dress up and play the part we do, we put it back in the closet until the next time we need it. The problem that creates the issue with following after Jesus is that we are all sinners. The Bible tells us in Romans 3:23, *"for all have sinned and fallen short of the glory of God"(NIV)*. Paul tells us the same truth in his letter to the church in Rome in two more places. First, Romans 3:10 tells us, *"As it is written: "There is no one righteous, not even one;" (NIV)*, and second in Romans 3:12, *"All have turned away, they have become worthless; there is no one who does good, not even one"(NIV)*.

17

Understanding that truth helps us realize that it is hard-wired into our hearts for us to rebel against God. You see that in the third chapter of the Bible. In Genesis chapters one and two, we get the story of the creation of the universe and everything in it. We even see that our purpose was to have a relationship with God. Yet Adam and Eve's lack of trust in God resulted in them thinking that God was keeping something from them. That God did not have their best interest at heart. Even though he placed them in charge of this world, they thought they could be equal to the creator of the universe.

This root of sin is deeply established in our souls. It is why we all struggle with the simple choice of doing what we want over what God commands. The effect of this is separation from God, and the penalty is death. Isaiah 59:2:" *But your iniquities have separated you from your God; your sins have hidden his face from you, so that he will not hear" (NIV)*. Romans 6:23 also tells us, *"For the wages of sin is death, but the gift of God is eternal life in Christ Jesus our Lord"(NIV)*. God's words clearly show us the high cost of our rebellion.

I have heard it said that anything you say in front of the word "but" does not matter. However, in the bible, this word helps us address the problem, and it helps give you the answer. Look at the verse from Romans 6:23. It starts with the issue: sin has a price: death. If it stopped right there, it would be very hopeless, but at the same time, very accurate. The "but," however, is the good news. We have a debt we can't pay. God is offering us forgiveness and eternal life through the life, death, and resurrection of his son Jesus. Christians call that truth "The Gospel" because it is good news for everyone. Jesus paid for our sins by taking our punishment on the cross. In return, he takes his righteousness (right standing with God) and places it on us.

Stained Glass Mascrade

It is well-known that the lives portrayed by people on social media do not accurately show that person's life. The pictures or videos we see have probably been edited and put through a few filters. Or some strategic editing in some strategic places. This inaccuracy between life on social media and life in the real world stood out when I saw a meme of Homer Simpson one day. It was Homer standing in his underwear, looking like he had been hitting the gym and was in good shape. Then they showed the back angle, and he had all the extra skin pinched up with clothes pens. People only show the good and try to hide the ugly angles of themselves. The truth we see on these platforms is what people want you to see.

Nobody wants to put a bad picture of themselves out for everyone to judge. Some people live on social media solely to judge everyone and everything. I witnessed this truth play out in front of me when I had to get all of my students (7th graders) to approve their names for the yearbook. They could care less about the names; it was the picture they were looking at. There were two types of responses: the first was "I look good," and the other was something like, "Ewww, I look horrible." We may not try to or want to admit it, but we care how people perceive us.

Our perception of ourselves goes deeper than our focus on our physical appearance. We can also compare economic stats or our relationship appearance. When we see posts about people buying new things or going on vacations, we can put ourselves down. This form of judgmental thinking can also cause resentment in relationships. Why doesn't my wife or husband love me like this person's husband or wife does? Or why do they not do those things for me? You need to remember deception is in perception. I have witnessed people on social media having an incredible relationship and being so in love. Then, six months or so later, they are separated and go through a divorce. Things aren't always as they seem, so we must carefully choose the correct lens through which we view our lives.

This issue has been going on long before social media entered the picture. The scary thing is that this same issue occurs at church. We hear someone pray and say to ourselves, why can we pray like that? Or maybe you walk in and ask someone how they are, and they respond with something like this; "I am just blessed, man; I just got a promotion at work, the kids are doing great, and we are building a house on the river. Yeah Man God is good all the time". When you hear those things, all you can think is that I just had to scream at my kids to get them in the car and get to church on time. Or if we are honest, close to being on time.

Parents, we have all been there. It is just a season, so keep bringing the kids to church. If you miss the first few songs or the welcome, I promise it's okay. God wants you there even if you are flustered and stressed. You are not alone! Sometimes, just walking through the doors is a victory. We hear churches say come as you are, but we are scared to do that. God's word is clear; he meets us just as we do.

We sometimes put on a show or "masquerade" at church. I think the honest reason for this is being "real" is problematic. Sometimes, we are ashamed of who we are or how we have been living. Admitting that to ourselves and others is a hard thing to do. We naturally don't like or lean towards hard things. We are like water. Water will always take the path of least resentence. Water makes up more than 70% of our brain and heart. Knowing this truth, it makes sense that we tend to travel the path of least resistance. In the aspect of the church, the path of least resistance is acting like you have it all together. If I just "play the part," I can make it through the ninety-minute service.

Part of this behavior stems from giving underserving people judgmental power over us. We miss out on some blessings of a relationship with God because we worry about what the people around us will think. Worrying like that is especially true in a small-town church. We never truly get lost in the presence of God during worship because we worry about the person beside or behind us judging our singing. Or we fight the urge to work some things out at the altar because we don't want people whispering about what's happening in our lives.

Even worse is when we allow this thought process to keep us from entering the church. Sometimes, the path of least resistance is avoidance. I have had people tell me they won't come to church because they are scared of judgment from people. Now we know God is omnipresent. We also know you don't have to be in a church building to experience him. The thing with the church is that you are not walking through it alone. You are surrounded by imperfect people chasing after a perfect God. That's why it is vital to show up just as we are.

I fear that while we all play the masquerade game at church, we become a stumbling block for others. We portray the church as a cathedral for the saints, instead showing them that it is a hospital for sinners. The one person (Jesus) who has the actual power to judge said he came not to judge but to save (John 3:17 *"For God did not send his Son into the world to condemn the world, but to save the world through him."* (NIV). If we portray our church as full of happy, good-looking people who look like they have their life together, then who honestly thinks they could fit in there? It would be easy for someone to feel their life should look like a stained-glass window when it looks like a Jackson Pollock painting. There is no point in showing up when you think you don't belong.

Attendance

According to church trac (2024), only 20% of Americans attend church weekly, while they report 51% report seldom or never attending a religious service. They also state that millennials have a higher attendance percentage than Gen X and the baby boomers. They pulled this information from the Barna group and the Gallop poll. This information gives a fair representation of the nation in 2024 and years past. However, the goal of this project is not to stop the masquerade so that church attendance will increase. No, the goal of every follower of Christ should be to grow the kingdom of heaven. Heaven and hell are real destinations! Not only are they real, but they are forever. It must become a desire to complete Jesus's great commission and spread the good news. Do you honestly want anyone to go to eternal damnation?

So, it is a double-edged sword. As followers of Jesus, our goal can't only be to have a room full of people to say we have a room full of people. On the flip side of that, though, it is about people. Part of the great commission is to make disciples to the ends of the Earth. I am no expert, but if you go to the ends of the earth, you will come across many people from all different walks of life. So, numbers are essential. The question is not how many we have, but how many have we told the good news to put their faith in Jesus? Eight billion people in the world that the bible tells us are all sinners. Because of that sin, those 8 billion people will die. How do I know that you might ask? The last time I checked, ten out of ten people died, and I never claimed to be smart, but 100% is good odds. So, they must hear the gospel to ensure they have their forever settled.

Bits and Pieces

We like to do things a bit backward as Christians. We believe that we rebelled against the holy God. We also believe that the same holy God who created the universe loves us enough to send his only son to pay for our sins. Not so he could brag or hold it over our heads that he bailed us out. We believe God did it because God loves and cares for us. He wants us! Let that truth sink in your heart and brain momentarily; the King of kings wants us. Even after believing and professing all that, we pick apart his word.

We cling to the scripture that makes us feel good, but we run from the scripture that convicts us. Most of us are ok with a convicting sermon now and then. If it happens too much or our toes start getting stepped on too often, we may move to the church down the street that preaches only more warm and fluffy parts of the Bible. Remember, we like the path of least resistance. To change a river's flow, you must build a dam. That requires lots of work moving earth and rock from one spot to another. The same will happen in your life when you follow after Jesus. Sin has a way of building up walls between God and us. There will be some things we have to change in our lives if we are to look more like him.

The issue with this is that if we only follow the parts of Jesus's teachings that we like, we aren't following Jesus of the bible. We are serving a God that we made. That will only lead to hurt and heartbreak.

22

Not to mention missing out on the blessing of being a part of the story of God. It is about knowing God and being known by him. Jesus tells us this truth in Matthew 7:21-23 "*21 "Not everyone who says to me, 'Lord, Lord,' will enter the kingdom of heaven, but only the one who does the will of my Father who is in heaven. 22 Many will say to me on that day, 'Lord, Lord, did we not prophesy in your name and in your name drive out demons and in your name perform many miracles?' 23 Then I will tell them plainly, 'I never knew you. Away from me, you evildoers!'"* It is not about works but about a relationship with God.

So, if we believe Jesus is the highest authority and he says go and make disciples, we are called to do just that. The thing with a command from someone in authority is that there is no wiggle room. If the general orders a code red. Then, the code read is carried out. If you don't understand that reference, watch "A Few Good Men." When we follow that command that Jesus gives us, we get to be his hands and feet and deliver the good news. You may not be called to long-term mission work, but we're all called. God may call you to go to the end of your street to share the gospel. At the same time, God may call you to share at the end of town. Then, you will have that group God calls to share the gospel to the ends of the earth. The point is the destination does not determine the calling. We are all called. The question is, where or to whom are we called to share with?

So, keeping it real in the streets is so important for followers of Jesus. We get to be the bearers of the good news of God's redeeming love while also showing the world glimpses of his mercy and grace through our lives. Remember, our most significant platform to share Jesus with the world is how you live your life.

Chapter 3

Denial

Mark 14:29-31 " 29 Peter declared, "Even if all fall away, I will not." 30 "Truly I tell you," Jesus answered, "today—yes, tonight— before the rooster crows twice[a] you will disown me three times." 31 But Peter insisted emphatically, "Even if I have to die with you, I will never disown you." And all the others said the same (NIV)."

Peter is one of my favorite people in the bible. I can see myself in his shoes, and I could also see myself responding to situations the way he did. I don't like to admit it, but it's the truth. Out of all of Jesus's followers, Peter had some of the highest highs. He was there on the mountain when Jesus showed him a glimpse of his glory. Peter was the disciple who exited the boat and walked on water with Jesus. He was in the room when Jesus raised Jairus's daughter. Peter was even at the tomb when Jesus called Lazarus out of it. Not to mention all of the behind-the-scenes things Peter got to be a part of. When Jesus taught a crowd, Peter could ask him what the lesson meant. I can imagine that getting to experience those moments had to be a spiritual experience like no other.

Peter even has one of the greatest professions of Jesus ever recorded right before Jesus rebuked him. Matthew tells us in his gospel that when Jesus and his disciples came into Caesarea Phillippi, he asked them a simple question: Who do people say I am? After they answer his question, Jesus asks them one of the most crucial questions of their lives and ours. Who do you say that I am? Peter answered him in Matthew 16:16: *"Simon Peter answered, "You are the Messiah, the Son of the living God." (NIV)*. I hope and pray we can answer that question just like Peter did.

On the flip side of that coin, Peter also had some of the lowest lows. Yes, Peter did get to walk on water, but he sank because of his fear and doubt. Peter even got called Satan by Jesus because he said he would never go to the cross. He was good at sticking his foot in his mouth. Look at what he tells Jesus in Matthew 16:21-23 *"21 From that time Jesus began to show his disciples that he must go to Jerusalem and suffer many things from the elders and chief priests and scribes, and be killed, and on the third day be raised. 22 And Peter took him aside and began to rebuke him, saying, "Far be it from you, Lord! This shall never happen to you." 23 But he turned and said to Peter, "Get behind me, Satan! You are a hindrance to me. For you are not setting your mind on the things of God, but on the things of man"* (NIV).

I don't know about you, but I can easily relate to this passage. Peter hears the person he just called the messiah's plan and pulls him aside to say no. It is easy to be an armchair quarterback and say I would never do that. I want to challenge you to reflect on your life and think of all your time advising God. We all have done it. Remember, as much time as you spend talking to God, spend at least that much time listening to him.

Camp Vibes

Camps are always a highlight of every youth ministry. If you have gotten to experience them, you know what I am talking about. The first night is always a feeling-out process. You have some students who come to camp fired up. They are always the ones worshiping the first service. Then you have some students who are used to being in church, but they are acting cool. Then you have the ones who never come to anything other than youth, who feel like a fish out of water. Then, after a week, the students seemed to have a change of heart. The fun games, late nights, and diets of high carbs and sugar are not the reason for the change of heart. That change of heart is due to the fact they interact with the Holy Spirit multiple times a day. They get taken out of their life where they may not have been living for the Lord, and they get to focus entirely on Jesus. You can not spend time focusing on Jesus and not leave changed.

By the end of camp, the vibe in the room is always different. Some students in the group who were too cool for worship now worship without regard for who is around them. Students who had no clue who Jesus was at the start of the week now profess how much they love him. Some camps even have a testimony time at the last service. Now, this can be very powerful, and it can be very awkward. The main point of this part of camp is to let the students get up there and say they are changed. Some even promise they will never return to the old ways again.

The hard part of living out those promises made at camp for some is that everyday life has a different energy than camp. Where you were going to church twice a day at camp, it drops back down to twice a week—or, in some cases, not at all. The time you spend with Jesus gets filled with other things. We break all our promises to the Lord after a few weeks back home. Now, I know that it is not everyone's story, but it is mine.

I was one of those students at camp. I knew who Jesus was and that he was my savior. In the summer of my 10th-grade year, I felt God calling me to preach. I remember listening to the pastor at camp and feeling God speak in my heart that he created to preach the word. When I was little, my mom always told me I would either be a preacher or president because of how I could talk. I guess mamas just have a way of knowing these things. I wrestled with the reality of that calling for a few months but eventually surrendered my life to God's call. So now, I am 16 years old and starting to preach to my youth group and other churches. However, I broke all of those promises I made.

I Don't know Him

Peter's actions on the night of Jesus's arrest and trial are very different from the ones where he called him Christ, the son of God. Before we dive into the scripture, I want to set the stage for you. The events of Jesus' arrest and trial are all happening at night. The religious elite plotted to take Jesus of Nazareth out of the picture. Jesus and his disciples went to the garden of Gethsemane after the Passover dinner. It was in the garden a mob of religious leaders and men came to find Jesus. It was at that moment when Judas, one of Jesus's disciples, betrayed him. Thinking with his heart instead of his brain, Peter tried to stop this from happening and struck the high priest servant in the ear with a sword. Jesus was under arrest, and he still rebuked Peter and reattached the high priest's servant's ear. Then Jesus is led away to stand trial.

Let's pick the story up in Luke's gospel. Luke 22:54-62 *54 Then seizing him, they led him away and took him into the house of the high priest. Peter followed at a distance. 55 And when some there had kindled a fire in the middle of the courtyard and had sat down together, Peter sat down with them. 56 A servant girl saw him seated there in the firelight. She looked closely at him and said, "This man was with him." 57 But he denied it. "Woman, I don't know him," he said. 58 A little later someone else saw him and said, "You also are one of them." "Man, I am not!" Peter replied. 59 About an hour later another asserted, "Certainly this fellow was with him, for he is a Galilean." 60 Peter replied, "Man, I don't know what you're talking about!" Just as he was speaking, the rooster crowed. 61 The Lord turned and looked straight at Peter. Then Peter remembered the word the Lord had spoken to him: "Before the rooster crows today, you will disown me three times." 62 And he went outside and wept bitterly (NIV).*

How Peter acted the night of Jesus' arrest differs significantly from when Jesus entered Jerusalem at the start of the week. Look at how Matthew describes the scene of Jesus' entry. We find it in Matthew 21:6-9 *"6 The disciples went and did as Jesus had instructed them. 7 They brought the donkey and the colt and placed their cloaks on them for Jesus to sit on. 8 A very large crowd spread their cloaks on the road, while others cut branches from the trees and spread them on the road.* **9** *The crowds that went ahead of him and those that followed shouted, "Hosanna to the Son of David!" "Blessed is he who comes in the name of the Lord!" "Hosanna in the highest heaven!"(NIV).* This type of entrance was what you would see from a conquering king entering the city.

It does not tell us how the disciples felt or acted that day. I could imagine a feeling of awe coming over them. Or the disciples may feel extreme pride for being his followers. They may have walked a little taller that day, as Squintz did after kissing the lifeguard in The Sandlot. However, Peter acted that day. It would be a safe bet to say it drastically differed from his actions a few days later.

We do the same thing in our lives. It is easy to proclaim Jesus when everyone around you is doing the same thing. Would you still follow if no one else was? This thought came to me when I went to a movie one night and was the only one in the theater. God hit me in the heart with this question. If no one else in the world was going after me, would you? It is easy to say yes but realize that your answer and commitment level will be tested.

Reasons

Why would Peter deny Jesus? That is an honest question for all of us to ask. Not why would Peter, but why would we? It is not like he did not know what would happen to Jesus. Jesus told them this throughout the lead-up to the Passover feast in Jerusalem. Some possible factors that could have played into Peter's actions that night will help us understand why we deny Jesus in certain situations. We will look at fear, peer pressure, and panic in Peter's situation. Then, we will examine the same reasons later in our own story.

The first potential reason we will look at is fear. Peter would have known that the religious leaders did not like Jesus. Remember, they had already tried to stone him once. Peter also could have remembered what happened to Jesus' cousin, John for standing up to the leaders of the time. Naturally, Peter could have been scared that he would soon join Jesus in chains and possibly in death. In psychology, they call it the fight or flight mentality. We have a higher chance of survival if we run from what could hurt us. So, Peter's response that night was flight. He did not physically run away like the others. Yet his actions ran away from Jesus.

The second reason that could have caused Peter's denial that night was peer pressure. On this night, when those with power held Jesus as a prisoner, it would have created a different feeling for the disciples from when he entered the city. None of the gospel accounts say people protested for Jesus's release. We see the opposite when the Jewish leaders encouraged the release of another man instead of Jesus. Some of this is because it happened at night and early in the morning. All that was done by design, so they did not have to deal with the public. Remember that the public greeted him as a king at the beginning of the week. No matter the case, Peter blended in with the crowd by denying Jesus. It is hard to stand alone or to go against the grain. Peer pressure gets you to look just like everyone else.

The last possible reason I could see for Peter's denial of Jesus would be Panic. During panic attacks, webmd.com reports that the different parts of our brain that are tied to fear become more active during attacks. Another way to say it is that staying calm in the chaos is challenging. You could easily describe that night as chaotic for the followers of Jesus. Their rabbi, whom they had seen walk on water, heal the sick, and raise the dead, is now considered an enemy of the state.

Matthew tells us in his gospel that Jesus predicted Peter's denial just hours before the events occurred. Peter said he would follow Jesus to the grave even if everyone else fell away. I know Peter's heart was in the right place, but his actions that night did not back up his promise. Not only did he say I don't know Jesus, but he started calling down curses for people saying he did. Maybe it was because of fear, peer pressure, or panic. It would be easy to sit back and judge, but when I look back on parts of my life, I realize that I did the same thing for many of the same reasons.

29

Parking Lot

My teenage years in Alabama were a blast. Most of my memories could have been scenes from a country music video. I even remember going mud riding after church one Sunday in one of my friends' Toyota Tacoma. Just like in a country song, we got stuck. Sitting on a tailgate in a field was not out of the norm. Growing up where I did and with the people, I was with was a blessing.

One of the things that stands out to me is how much time we spent in parking lots. Every school had a parking lot where kids would meet up and hang out. Ours was in the parking lot of an old grocery store. I watched people fight, fall in and out of love, and even hit golf balls across the road. That's not even mentioning the illegal things I witnessed in those parking lots. My friends would either drink in the parking lot or come to the parking lot after drinking. As we got a little older, people's choices became more questionable. The activities that took place by the people around me became more troublesome.

I can honestly say that by the grace of God, I never got into the drinking or drug scene. Just because I did not do it did not mean I was not around it. From experience, when people find out you don't drink, they love it. Because they know they will always have a sober driver. I would love to say I stood out from the crowd, but that would be a lie. The only difference between them and me was, I was sober. That was the first way I was denying Jesus.

That was pointed out to me by a friend one night in that parking lot. She was making some of those bad choices the crowd was making. I don't remember how it started, but I will remember this conversation for the rest of my life. My friend looked at me dead in my eyes and called me a hypocrite. That is hard for anyone to hear. The worst thing about it was she was 100% correct. Yes, I was not drinking, smoking, or having sex, but I looked and talked like everyone else. I am ashamed of that. I would love to rationalize or make excuses for it, but I can't. I never said I didn't know Jesus, but my actions looked like I had never met him.

No one is perfect is a true statement. Honestly, I could have been better in that parking lot. Or I could have avoided it altogether. Fitting in was more important to me during those years. Some of you might be wondering what the big deal is. You were not sleeping around, and you were not drinking or doing drugs. The problem was that I was not keeping it real. Looking back on my life, I see multiple times when I looked more like the world than I looked like Jesus. The world considered me a good guy, but I know I was not pointing people to Jesus. I knew where the line was. I knew what I could do and still be considered a good guy. Jesus said in Matthew 5:14, *"You are the light of the world. A town built on a hill cannot be hidden." (NIV)*. I trusted Jesus with my salvation, but my light for him was dim.

Tell me Why

If you look back on your life or take a look at your current life, it might look like mine did that night. You said you were a follower of Jesus, but your actions looked/seemed drastically different. If we reflect on the events, we might be able to see some of the causes for our denial. While there could be many reasons for our actions, I want to examine them through the possible causes we look at for Peter's denial.

The first is fear. We can make bad choices from a state of fear. What are we scared of? Death is an obvious choice. I believe fear of death could have been an emotion that Peter could have felt the night of his denial. The fear of death is also something Christians face today around the world. This fear could stop you from walking on the path God has for you. Nobody willingly wants to die for something that does not mean anything to them. So, we must ask ourselves, is following Jesus worth losing our life?

Another choice is fear of rejection. Fear of rejection is brutal in our teenage years and into our twenties. We naturally want to fit in. Following Jesus will have you making choices the people around you do not choose. Our choices can be one of the biggest platforms to tell people that Jesus is the only way. Yes, the world will likely reject you

31

the more you look like Jesus. When they see that by following Jesus, you have pure joy, it will lead them to ask why. Why are you happy even though the world rejects you? This is always one of the best ways to share your faith. That question of why you are different easily flows into talking about Jesus. Remember that the things of this world only lead to destruction. So, everyone who goes after those things will always come up empty, and we have the answer that could fill their heart.

The last one is the fear of missing out. We feel we are missing out on something by doing what God says. Fear of missing out was the same fear Eve had in the garden when Satan tempted her. That goes back to trusting God. Are we trusting he is not keeping something better from us? Can you say you believe he has your best interest at heart with his commands and calling on your life? We must remember that the things and experiences of this world will pale in comparison to the glory of standing with Jesus in the future.

The second possible cause of denying Jesus is peer pressure. Most of the time, there is no pressure to say you don't know Jesus, but there is pressure to live like you don't know him. Looking back at my story, I see that exact scenario plays out. The night in the parking lot, no one was openly saying they didn't know Jesus. I never heard anyone ask if I knew Jesus on any of those nights. They did not have to. My actions answered the question for me. Those decisions I made were built off the fear of rejection by my peers.

I have also found in my own life that when you start deciding to live for Jesus when others are not, they will pressure you, even more to live like them. I remember people getting mad at me in college when they found out I did not drink or have sex. Some of them got physically mad at me. That reaction from people probably happened out of guilt. We know when we are living wrong. We don't like being alone in that shame and guilt. So, we naturally compare ourselves to people doing worse things than we are. Then, based on those criteria, we try to tell ourselves we are not that bad. If everyone else did it or worse, that would somehow make what we did not as wrong.

Finally, the last reason we are going to look at for the denial of Jesus is panic. When we give into panic, we can make bad choices. It can lead us to seek shelter in things other than God—choices we would not usually make in calm situations. Panic is the exact opposite of what God wants us to do. Psalm 46:10 tells us, "He says, *Be still, and know that I am God; I will be exalted among the nations, I will be exalted in the earth. (NIV)*". Being still is trusting who God is. Panic does not always have to do with fear. Panic could come from choosing something you know does not glorify God because you think you will never get that chance again. Whatever the reason, panic can lead us to deny Jesus with our words and actions.

When I look back at the moments when I was denying Jesus with my words or actions, I could see one or all three of these feelings at play in my heart and mind. As you look back at the moments you remember denying Jesus, you can see the causes or feelings that led to your denial. Understanding why we did it can help us to avoid doing it the next time. It is like when a coach gives you a scouting report on your opponent. The more you know what they want to do, the better you can execute during the game.

You may need to ask yourself, has Jesus been the king of your life? We love Jesus as our savior, but are we basing our decisions on him being the highest authority in our lives? If Jesus is our king, then we must follow his instructions. You may not have felt these three stressors, but other feelings could have caused your denial. I wanted to point these out to help you know when you sense these feelings coming, you will know it's time to pray. Jesus also told his disciples in the garden on the night of his arrest. *"Watch and pray so that you will not fall into temptation. The spirit is willing, but the flesh is weak."* Matthew 26:41(NIV).

That is sound advice for us as well. We need to watch and pray as we go out into the world. We must also remember that no matter how much we want to follow Jesus, our flesh is weak. So, we need help from the Holy Spirit to avoid temptation. We are lucky because our savior

33

knows how to face temptation. He also lets us lean on his strength and understanding in times of trouble or temptation.

Chapter 4

Broken Cisterns

Jeremiah 2:13 "My people have committed two sins: They have forsaken me, the spring of living water, and have dug their own cisterns, broken cisterns that cannot hold water (NIV)."

Having the right priorities in life is essential. Attention and time are the by-products of your priorities. Attention and time are not unlimited. So, you have to decide what deserves your attention and time. The same is true for organizations. They focus and spend time on things they care about. What you prioritize and care about will get the focus of your mind. It will also get the attention of your heart. What has your heart will always be what has you. We set ourselves up for failure when we focus on things counterproductive to our priorities. It would be like trying to store water in a broken bucket. It won't work, and you will have a mess to clean up.

We hear this exact truth from the prophet Jeremiah in Jeremiah 2:13: *"My people have committed two sins: They have forsaken me, the spring of living water, and have dug their own cisterns, broken cisterns that cannot hold water.* When we deny Jesus, we reject him as our king. We saw this play out in both Peter's and my story of denial. Why would anyone deny Jesus after they have confessed him as savior and lord? That is what we will look at and address in this chapter. You may or may not have any stories of living like a hypocrite, but there is a chance you have forsaken him by where you placed your faith, time, or attention. Faith set

35

anywhere other than God is like holding water in a broken bucket. For example, no matter how much you believe, it won't work.

You may not have little statues of different Gods around your house, like a mini-Buddha on the nightstand or a Zeus statue in your garden. However, we can have idols that we may not even realize. Merriam-Webster tells us that an Idol is an image or representation of a god used as an object of worship or an object of extreme devotion. When I read that definition, I think of college football. Being from Alabama, I understand people are devoted and sometimes even worship football teams and players. So, think about the things in your life that that definition describes. Could you look to money, friends, loved ones, careers, accolades, or possessions in this way? Remember, faith placed in these things will always leave you with a mess to clean up.

Take and Take and Take

We see multiple examples of people looking to idols in the bible. One of the more well-known examples is the story of Elijah and the prophets of Baal. You can find this story in 1st Kings chapter 18, but I will catch you up quickly. Elijah confronts King Ahab about his worship of Baal. Elijah's point was to prove who the one true God was. So, the 450 followers of Baal and Elijah built separate altars. They placed a sacrifice on the altars and said whichever God brought down fire from the sky to consume the sacrifice placed on the altar would be the true God. Elijah let the Baal followers go first. The 450 Baal followers danced, yelled, and even cut themselves all morning; nothing happened. In the end, they were left tired, bleeding, and empty. Believing in a god who did not show up.

They had given their life for something that they looked to for security and comfort. Only to end up realizing that their faith and hope had been misplaced. When the fire fell after Elijah prayed to God, I would bet many heads were hanging. If not, then I am sure they were when Elijah told the people to put them to death. Their idol had taken more than it gave. Another way to say it is that it cost them more than

36

it was worth. For the priests of Baal, it cost them their lives. Take a look at your life for a moment. Is there something that is getting your devotion or your worship? Is it taking more than it gives?

Everything has a price. It will cost you financially, physically, mentally, spiritually, or in many cases, it will cost you parts of each. We should not be surprised by this reality. Jesus told us about the devil's plans in John 10:10: *"The thief comes only to steal and kill and destroy; I have come that they may have life and have it to the full. (NIV)"*. While the things of the world may give us instant gratification, the lifetime of effects it will cause far outweighs what it provides. Make no mistake, the things of this world will cost you. The price is eternal separation from God.

One day in class, I had a similar conversation with my students about how something can cost you more than it is worth. In 2024, vaping is an issue our youth are facing. Kids want their peers to see them as cool, so what do they do? They bring the vapes to school. I can't say that all parents are not condoning this action but let us pretend that all parents tell their kids not to do it. Parents love their kids and want the best for them. If the kids know that and willingly decide to deny what their parents have told them and look to other things, could this not be a form of denial?

Stress, anxiety, or trying to fit in could be reasons for the behavior. Most of the time, those bad habits end up causing more stress or anxiety than you had before falling into those habits. You may have an example of that in your own life when a habit or hang-up caused more problems than it solved. We don't always know what things are best for us. James tells us this truth in chapter 1:5 when he says, *"If any of you lacks wisdom, you should ask God, who gives generously to all without finding fault, and it will be given to you. (NIV)"* This does not say to ask for wisdom so you can be more intelligent than everyone else, but to ask for wisdom to follow God more closely.

Rewards

We understand the results we will get when we look to things other than God. Now, let us look at why we run to those things in the first place. By understanding the why or what you are looking for from these things, you can recenter your attention and focus on the only place you can get any of the following things. In case you have missed it up till now, the place we need to look is God. James 1:17 tells us this very truth: *"Every good and perfect gift is from above, coming down from the Father of the heavenly lights, who does not change like shifting shadows. (NIV)"*.

God is our good heavenly father, and he never changes. He was good yesterday, he is good today, and he will be good tomorrow! Earlier, we looked at Satan's intentions. He comes to kill, steal, and destroy. We know the things of this world are from Satan. Knowing that, does looking at things in this world for comfort, security, or peace make sense to you? It would be like letting someone convicted of human trafficking babysit your child. That would be a bad life choice.

#1 Comfort

The first reason people can look to idols or things other than God is for comfort. We are all created and designed to seek comfort and stability. They use the term homeostasis to describe this action in science. Britannica.com says homeostasis is "any self-regulating process by which biological systems tend to maintain stability while adjusting to conditions that are optimal for survival." Discomfort in our situation propels us to seek comfort in other places. For example, you naturally look for a replacement if you have an uncomfortable chair. We will look to other things to see if our situation or circumstances are not ideal. It goes further than that; when relationships get awkward, we look to escape instead of working on the problem. This type of behavior is why the divorce rate is so high. In those situations, the price is paid not only by the adults but also by the kids who will now grow up in single-parent homes. Remember, our actions can have ripple effects on the ones around us.

We must remember that Jesus never said it would be easy to follow him. Jesus tells us it was actually the opposite in Matthew 16:24 when he said: ***"Then** Jesus said to his disciples, "Whoever wants to be my disciple must deny themselves and take up their cross and follow me (NIV)."* So, if the one who says "follow me" tells you that it won't be easy, then don't be foolish enough to think that this journey of Christianity will be a walk in the park. I look at it like Navy SEAL training. To earn the trident, you must go through BUDs (basic underwater demolition training). It is challenging during the process, but the end goal is worth it. The same statement rings true about following Jesus. However, we don't earn our right standing with God like Navy SEALs earn their trident. Jesus gave us that right by what he did on the cross! We must remember that our struggles now will pale in compassion for the joy of standing with Jesus in his glory when he returns.

Remembering that Jesus cares about what we are going through is essential. Not only does he care, but he also understands. Jesus being 100% human is vital because our savior understands the struggle. Jesus faced temptation just like we do. Yet he did not run to things to give him comfort or reprieve. We see this in the account of Jesus's temptation in the wilderness. He was presented with the option of food and power, and he responded to the temptation with the word of God. If he had given in, Jesus would have received instant gratification. Yet honoring God in the discomfort was more important than temporary relief from his situation. We urgently need to take note of Jesus' response. He shows us how to fight our battles. It is also worth noting that we can find true comfort in the word of God.

#2 Security

The second reason we could deny Christ and turn to idols is security. We are prone to quickly forget all God has done and look for safety in other things. We see this example in the story of Moses and the golden calf in Exodus chapter 32. God had led his people out of bondage. Now, they were in a season of waiting. They were on the journey but not at the destination. Moses was meeting with God on Mount Sanai. It was there that God gave him the law and instructions. While Moses was gone for a long time, the people God had rescued became impatient. They thought Moses was never returning and asked Aaron to make them gods that would go before them and take care of them. Now, to make this god so they could be safe, they had to give up their gold jewelry. They were willing to give up something valuable for something that could give them nothing in return.

My daughter is a prime example of this kind of behavior. She has two stuffed foxes that are like her security blanket. Everywhere she goes, we have to have a big foxy and little foxy. Most little kids exhibit this kind of behavior as well. They find something to cling to. She does not know that the two toys offer her nothing in return. They can't protect her or provide for her. So why does she always want them with her? I think it's because it's something she can physically touch or hold when her anxiety goes up.

The need for physical touch is a basic human need, according to a Psychological Today article posted in 2021. Believing you are safe because you can physically touch something does not require great faith. That is why some people have problems following Jesus. The Bible teaches us there is a blessing in believing without seeing. We find that in Jesus's conversation with Thomas after his resurrection in John 20:29, *"Then Jesus told him, "Because you have seen me, you have believed; blessed are those who have not seen and yet have believed (NIV)."*

You probably do not have a golden calf in your house that you pray to or rub when things start to get sideways. However, You might look to the stock market or your 401k to give you peace. Or your career or accolades get all of your attention and focus. Your social media likes and views could make you feel like everything is ok. If that's you, I want to warn you that you could be propping up false idols in your life. Look what God said to Moses about the people who clung to the idol in Genesis 32:33: *"**The** Lord replied to Moses, "Whoever has sinned against me I will blot out of my book." (NIV)*. Our security should come from our salvation and our name in the Book of Life, not in things of this world that will pass away.

#3 Peace

No one likes that uneasy feeling in your stomach when you are unsure what will happen. When you are in school, that sick feeling can come from when you don't know if that certain someone likes you. Or if you are waiting to see if you will make the team. When we get older, we can have the same feelings in the pit of our stomach. When your boss calls you into their office. When something breaks in the house, and you have no idea where you will go, get the money to fix it. These are just a few examples of what can cause that sinking feeling in your gut. When you have kids, you live with that feeling 24/7.

Jesus is the only place we can find true peace. Peace from the things of the world is fleeting—here today and gone tomorrow. I can't help but think of people's responses after the stock market crash in 1929. I remember reading stories in history books about people who lost everything and ended up taking their own lives. When the thing they trusted to give them peace of mind let them down, they had nothing to fall on. Don't be fooled, falling and hitting rock bottom hurts.

Jesus tells us we can find peace in him. Look at John 14:27 with me: *"**Peace** I leave with you; my peace I give you. I do not give to you as the world gives. Do not let your hearts be troubled and do not be afraid." (NIV).* Jesus is the Prince of Peace, so the peace that he gives you is pretty good. In His peace, our hearts can be calm rather than being troubled. We can also live courageously instead of living in fear. We should strive to live out the words in Isaiah 26:3, where he says, *"You will keep in perfect peace those whose minds are steadfast, because they trust in you." (NIV).*

Good Tools, Bad Gods

401k's, investing, titles, accolades, and social media are good tools to have and use in your life. I don't want you to think I am saying you should not have any of them. Or you have to live like they did in the pre-electricity days. These platforms can be great tools to help us build the kingdom of God. We must ask ourselves, are we making our kingdom or helping build God's? The Bible tells us our answer to that question in 1st Corinthians 10:31: " *So whether you eat or drink or whatever you do, do it all for the glory of God. (NIV)*". Focusing on these things with the idea of glorifying God through them changes how we approach

41

these different tools. We will always find our hearts empty if we go to these things for comfort, security, or peace. As we have seen earlier, the cost will always be more than the reward.

No matter how useful these tools are to us, they are worse gods. They can't add a single second to your life. They also don't know you on a personal level. Nor did they deliver you from the bondage of sin. While these tools can make this life easier, they cannot save you! Trusting in these things to save your life would be like grabbing a washing machine instead of a life jacket when drowning. The washing machine makes life easier but can't save you. Don't only trust in things you can see and touch. I implore you to trust in the God who walks on water. It is better to have someone on top of the water to pull you out when you are drowning than to grab things sinking with you.

So, how do we keep these things as tools and not prop them up as idols? It starts with our heart and the first commandment God gave Moses on that mountain. God told Moses in Exodus 20:3, *"You shall have no other gods before me. (NIV)"* Jesus tells us the same thing in Matthew 22:37-38 *"Jesus replied: "Love the Lord your God with all your heart and with all your soul and with all your mind.'[38 This is the first and greatest commandment. (NIV)"*. This commandment is the key to not running to idols by ensuring that there is nothing before God in our hearts. In the passage in Exodus 32, God tells Moses he is a jealous God.

Also, make sure you love God with all you have; when we do that, we will find proper security and comfort that can only come from our Father in heaven. This process occurs by dying daily to self and centering your heart on God. When we love God with all we have, we have nothing to give to other things. The more we fall in love with God, the less we want to love different things.

Plug The Leak

If you have been filling the water of your life in broken vessels, you don't have to continue living that way. The result of pouring water into broken vessels will always be a mess you must clean up. Remember, God is in the restoration business. God puts broken people back together for our good and his glory. Take some time to look and see if you have propped up idols in your life. If you do, then lay them at the feet of Jesus. Like the prodigal son, the first step is turning and returning to the father.

One of the issues you might be facing is thinking that your sin has damaged you beyond repair. Or that God fixed you once, and then you broke again, and you don't know if he will do it again. What is the point of getting repaired if you just get damaged again? If that's you, I want to remind you of the story of Jesus and the woman at the well found in John chapter 4. Jesus meets this woman with a bad history. Her decisions in her life have caused it to shatter into many pieces. Through an encounter with Jesus, she left the well-restored. She came with a life that was a mess and went away with a life overflowing with love for Jesus.

Jesus is the only one who can put pieces of our lives back together again. Our lives are different when we overflow with living water rather than empty from a leak. What makes an overflow different from a leak? The vessel remains full. The woman at the wells' interaction with Jesus shows us that even though your life is broken, you can leave this moment restored and overflowing. All it takes is an encounter with Jesus. Are you ready to meet him?

Chapter 5

Test Time

2nd Corinthians 5:10: "For we must all appear before the judgment seat of Christ, so that each of us may receive what is due us for the things done while in the body, whether good or bad (NIV)."

Some of the most dreaded words students can hear uttered by teachers worldwide are: "Get out a piece of paper and something to write with." Maybe just reading those words brings back a sense of dread and worry in your stomach. Deep down, you know what is coming next: a test. In my entire career in education, I have never had a group of kids get excited for test day. They may never say it with their mouth, but in their eyes, they are saying bad things that I can not print in a book about Jesus. Maybe it's not that bad, but they are unhappy about it. Most of the time, they gladly let you know their displeasure.

The dread or unhappiness results from the test's finality. Once you take the test, you are guaranteed a result. Your score is going to impact your grade one way or another. You may not like it or want to admit it, but grades matter. As lovely as it would be for us to be able to show up, do nothing, and pass, that is not how the world works. You need to have the grade at the end of the class to get the credit. It does not matter if you had perfect attendance or no behavior problems. If you end the year with a 59 average, then you fail.

What's an even worse form of test is one that is a surprise. Kids are better when they can plan and study. Give them a pop test, and you will see fear and panic sweep the room. There is no preparation they can do for a pop test. They entirely rely on whether they did what they should have done leading up to the test. It boils down to whether they were paying attention or not. If they focus in class, they usually do well. If they did not focus on the material and did what they wanted to do, then the outcome was something they did not wish to have.

I have good news and bad news for you today. The bad news is that if you have finished your time in school, you still have one pop test coming at some point in your life. You don't know when or where, but you know it is coming. The good news is that since you know it is coming at some point, you can focus on ensuring you are ready for it. My goal for this chapter is to present the information for the test that every person living will take one day. This test is not just pass or fail; it's life or death.

Under Pressure

Do you or did you struggle with test anxiety? I did a quick search, and it brought me to studies done by Lumen Learning. They show that nearly 40% of people deal with moderate to severe test anxiety. I tell you that to let you know that you are not alone if tests make you anxious. Viewing tests under the lens of "what happens if I fail" can create a lot of pressure for yourself. I know from experience. I felt that same pressure a few different times during my college career.

The first time I faced pressure from a test was when I was an undergrad at Jacksonville State University. JSU had an exam that every student had to pass before graduating. The name of the test was the English Competency Exam, or the ECE for short. The test was straightforward. They give you a topic, and you must write an essay by hand. You are only allowed three mistakes. There was a time in my life when writing was not always my friend. I struggled with writing papers throughout my time in college. I was great at the content but could have done better at the grammar portion. JSU only offered the test once a semester. So, in classic Drew Hall fashion, I waited till my last semester to attempt the test. I felt that pressure for weeks until the results came out.

My next encounter with test pressure was when I walked through the process of getting into graduate school. Because I was not the best student during my undergrad years, as reflected by my grade point average, I had to take a test to get accepted into graduate school. I chose to take the Millers' Analogy Test (MAT). The great thing about this was you could take it as many times as needed. The problem was you had to pay for each attempt. So, after my first two attempts, my parents thought I needed to study first and then try again. After weeks of preparing and practicing for the test, I passed with flying colors.

I felt extreme pressure in each situation because of the consequences I would face if I did not pass the test. If I failed the ECE, it would keep me in school for at least another semester. If I did not pass the MAT, it would keep me out of graduate school and the chance to live out a dream. The sun would still have risen the next day if I had not passed either test. So, I felt pressure, and yes, there were consequences for not passing, but it was not life or death. One day, all of us will feel the weight of that pressure. The Bible tells us in Romans 14:13, *"So then, each of us will give an account of ourselves to God"* (NIV). God does not give partial credit or grade on a curve. Life's biggest test is pass or fail.

Pressure is a Privilege

The term "pressure is a privilege" comes from the understanding that if you are in a pressured situation, you are privileged to be there. Now I know what you're thinking; I have never been under the pressure and stress of a problem and felt privileged to go through it. You would not be alone in that line of thinking. I felt the same way when dealing with the pressure of passing the college test. Looking back on it now, I realize that the pressure from the opportunity was a gift. I was blessed to have been able to go to college and have the chance to graduate from a fantastic university. I was also blessed to have the opportunity to live out my dream of coaching in college.

Life's final exam also allows us to consider pressure a privilege. Yes, there is a lot at stake with this exam (heaven and hell). The reality of the results is where the opportunity is found. None of us deserve to even have the chance to go to heaven. God is good, holy, loving, and kind. We were made in his image, yet the relationship was broken due to our sin. He gives us another chance because he loves us even though we messed it up. He gave us a path for us to be restored to him. This is where the privilege is found. We are not trying to live a life that earns favor with God. We are trying to live a life that honors him and builds his kingdom. We get to show Christ in us to the world.

The privilege is that no matter how many times or how bad you have screwed it up, if you have breath in your lungs, you have the chance to get it right. An opportunity is all anyone can ask for. Think about how meaningless life would be if we were doomed from the start with no way to make it right. Some people feel that is how the world works, but that is not how the story of God's goodness, glory, and grace is written.

Life's Pop Test

A quick Google search shows you have a 1 in 292.2 million chance to win the power ball lottery. Stacker.com says you have the odds of 1 in 15,300 being struck by lightning. It also says that you have a .3% chance of getting your car stolen. However, everyone has a 100% chance of something happening in life, and that is dying. It is a universally accepted fact that ten out of ten people die. At an FCA event, I once heard Mark Cahill say, "Every second, two people die." He also said, "By the time you go to bed tonight, 180,000 people will have taken their last breath on earth." That stat can get your attention real quick.

So that begs the question of what happens to us after we die. It is safe to assume you have asked yourself that question at least once. Religions and people around the world have different answers to that

47

question. They range from reincarnation (coming back as something or someone different) to nothing that happens after we die. Some believe in heaven and hell but disagree on how you get there. How you answer that question impacts how you live your life.

Many religions have different wordings, but most boil down to a cosmic deity that keeps score of what we do with our time on earth. That kind of thinking has its issues. What is the score that you have to reach to get to heaven? How do you know what gives or takes a point from you? If we don't understand how it works, we are all playing an unfair game. Could you imagine getting up before God and him telling you that you missed it by one point? That is not love but cruelty. Why would you want to worship a God like that? I had that exact conversation with a Muslim woman at a conference in Orlando. When I asked her those questions, she had no answers for me. As Christians, we have a different explanation of how to get to heaven.

All religious explanations of how to get to heaven are different, so there is no way they are all right. Every path does not lead to God. Jesus tells us this truth in Matthew 7:13-14 when he said, *"13 'Enter through the narrow gate. For wide is the gate, and broad is the road that leads to destruction, and many enter through it. 14 But small is the gate and narrow the road that leads to life, and only a few find it (NIV)."* Suppose there is a possibility that an answer is wrong. In that case, you must ensure you answer such an important question correctly. So, get out your paper and something to write with boys and girls. It's time to see if we are ready for the test.

Eternity Exam

Before we dive into the eternity exam, I will give you some directions. First, these questions come from what the bible tells us. If you don't believe in the God of the Bible or, as the Israelites call him, "Yahweh," then you will probably find issues with these questions. If that's you, I want you to know I am glad you are walking through this with me. By the end of this chapter, I pray you are 100% prepared for when you stand before God. For everyone else, this is to ensure you have the correct answer, not just an emotional experience.

First, let's start with some prerequisite questions. These are important to understand your view on God. Question number one is how we got here. Was the universe created, or did it happen from a big bang? Think about your time in life, science, or biology for a second. Those classes taught us that life is very complex. There is too much evidence of order in the universe to ignore. You can find entire books on how nature points to the intelligent design of a creator. If you believe in the Big Bang, ask yourself where the matter came from before the Big Bang. Something surely can't come from nothing. When deeply diving into these questions, you can see how our world points to a creator.

The second question has two parts, who is this creator, and is he good? People and different religions have been trying to answer that for centuries. A.W Tozer said in his book (The Knowledge of The Holy), *"What comes into our minds when we think about God is the most important thing about us."* The Bible tells us in Genesis that God created the heavens and the earth. If we believe the Bible, we agree that the God of the Bible is the creator of everything. So, we must ask ourselves, is he good? The Bible tells us in Isaiah chapter 6 that God is seated on the throne with seraphim circling him, saying to each other continually, "Holy, *holy, holy is the Lord Almighty."* Holy means set apart, so if six-winged creatures are circling God and calling him holy, it would be a safe bet to say he is good.

If God is good, then what are we? Or where do we stand compared to the Holy God? We saw that in Romans 3, we have all fallen short of the glory of God (Romans 3:23). Holy can't be unholy. So, we are born into and live in separation from God because of what the Bible calls sin. Sin is doing what we want over what God wants us to do. Or simply breaking the rules, God gave us to live by. Can you think of examples like that in your life? All it takes is one sin to separate us from God. We also saw in Romans that the wages of sin is death (Romans 6:23). If we die in sin, then we will forever be separated by that sin from

Holy God. That would lead us to the question, how do we return to right standing with God? The Bible also gives us that answer in John 3:16: "For *God so loved the world that he gave his one and only Son, that whoever believes in him shall not perish but have eternal life*" (NIV).

That brings us to the first question we must be ready to answer on life's most significant exam. Who is Jesus.? When we look at the last 2,000 years of human history, one name has defined all of history. So, who was this carpenter from Nazareth that is still being talked about today? Some people say he was a prophet. Others say he was a moral teacher. Only Christians give him the title of Lord. That is where the separation starts. It's easy to read the teachings of Jesus and call him good. Good teachers can't beat death, though. The bible tells us that Jesus was crucified and died for our sins. Jesus was buried in a tomb, and three days later, he got up, defeating sin and death. It would be foolish not to follow him if you believe he did all that. So here is your chance to answer the first question:

Who is Jesus?
A) He was a good guy and teacher who did some cool stuff, but he was not God and did not rise from the grave.
B) He is The Christ, The Messiah, The Son of God, The Way, The Truth, and The Life

The next question is even more important than the last. It has to deal with relationships, not just knowledge. That question is, what did you do with Jesus? Do we believe John 14:6 when it says, "*Jesus answered, 'I am the way and the truth and the life. No one comes to the Father except through me'*" (NIV). Or can we return to the right standing with God some other way? How you answer this question will guide the rest of your life. So how would you answer the question, and does your life match your answer?

What did you do with Jesus?
A) Reject him and live your way.

B) You believe you need Jesus to save you, but you live life your way. You never make Jesus the king of your life and keep him as cosmic fire insurance.

C) You believe in his life, death, and resurrection for salvation & follow him, and deny yourself by carrying your cross.

Understand there is a right and wrong answer. It is not about knowledge or acts of service. It is about a relationship.

EKG

An electrocardiogram, or EKG, tests the heart for different heart conditions. Suppose you might be having a heart attack; an EKG is how the doctors and nurses will check you. Life's eternal exam also examines our hearts. Salvation is not a paper test; you can hang it on the refrigerator, showing God you passed. Paul tells us in Romans 10:9 that "**If** you declare with your mouth, *"Jesus is Lord,"* and believe in your heart that God raised him from the dead, you will be saved*" (NIV). It is with our hearts that we answer life's two big questions.

The process starts with repentance. Repentance is a 180-degree turn from one thing to another. In terms of Christianity, it's turning from our sins and back to God. Then, we confess Jesus is who he said he was, "Lord." When we claim Jesus as Lord, we say he is Lord over all our lives. The second part is believing that Jesus died to pay for our sins on the cross and was raised from death by God. By doing that, the bible says you receive salvation from condemnation. It is not something you earn, but a gift God gives you.

Are you prepared to answer these questions before Holy God? You can know you are ready for these questions with a simple prayer. It is not the words that save you but the attitude of repenting from sin and turning your heart back to God. If you realize you are a sinner and have never put your faith in Jesus for your salvation, I want to invite you to do that with me today. Join me in this prayer: **"Dear God, I know I am a sinner. I know my sin separates me from you. Today, Lord, I repent and turn from my sin back to you. Save me**

today, Jesus, and be my King forever. In Jesus name, I pray, amen."

If you said that prayer and meant it in your heart, I want to be the first to congratulate you. You have gone from death to life. The Bible says you are a new creation. The old has gone, and the new has come. I encourage you to contact a local church to get plugged into a community of believers. God does not just want a moment of your life. Jesus is calling you to follow him. That's the beauty of the local church. We are getting to worship a perfect father with imperfect people like us. I want you to know a party in heaven is going on because of your decision. Focus on the impact of that and the eternal consequences for you. Let that joy fill your heart and worship the God who saves.

Chapter 6

Alarms

Joel 2:1: "Blow the trumpet in Zion; sound the alarm on my holy hill. Let all who live in the land tremble, for the day of the LORD is coming. It is close at hand—

I t does not matter where you went to school; everyone has some of the same shared experiences. Whether public or private, large or small, every school has safety plans. You may remember having them posted on the classroom wall somewhere. A school's safety plans include procedures to follow for fires, severe weather, and even evacuation plans. After the events of Columbine High School, schools around the country started putting in plans and procedures for active shooters/intruders.

Every year at the start of school, teachers and administrators take students through these drills in case the procedures must be activated due to an emergency. Some schools even go through these drills once a semester. Not only do schools practice the emergency plan, but they also go over the alarms for the plan. Whether the bell rings or a code call over the intercom system, these alarms alert you to quickly change your behavior and focus. Adhering to these warnings can be the difference between life and death.

Hard To Hear

In the last chapter, we walked through the gospel to ensure you understand Jesus is the only way to salvation. If you have yet to work through that or are struggling with that decision, take some time before going further on this journey to nail down where you put your faith. This chapter is for Christians and people who claim to be Christians. We will take a look at seven things Jesus knows. We will also discuss different things Jesus has against people who claim to be Christians but are not living for him, as well as warnings Jesus has for his followers.

We find all of this in the book of Revelation. That book at the end of the Bible that can be scary or hard to understand. You might even think it's weird. That's okay; you are not alone in that line of thought. These instructions and warnings we will look at are found in Jesus's letter to the seven churches in Asia Minor (Revelation 2-3). You may not be reading this book in Asia Minor (kudos if you are). Still, no matter our location, Jesus's words carry value for us today. I need you to know that some of these things will be hard to read and process. They were hard for me to process in my own life.

It is essential to understand that there is a price for living in opposition to Jesus or tolerating people in opposition to Jesus. So, think of this as an intervention. During an intervention, people read letters to tell you how your actions hurt others and yourself. Jesus is doing this for us in Revelations chapter 2-3. Remember that God is jealous for our hearts and wants all of us. Even if one or more warnings apply, you still have time to change. That's what this entire journey is about—learning how to live out our faith. So, if we are going to keep it real in the streets, we need to see if we have a behavior or, if you are like me, behaviors that need to change.

Seven things Jesus Knows

The first thing we see that Jesus knows about us comes from the letter to the church in Ephesus in Revelation 2. Jesus tells them he knows their deeds and patient endurance. He reiterates that by saying he knows that the church at Ephesus does not tolerate wicked people. Could Jesus say that about us? Do our deeds show patience and endurance to his teaching? There is nothing hidden from Jesus. He knows the intentions behind our deeds. Jesus does not listen to our lip service or our performance. He looks at our hearts. Another way to look at it is Jesus sees the why behind our actions.

The second thing we see Jesus knows about us comes from the letter to the church at Smyrna. Jesus tells them that he knows their afflictions and their suffering. Jesus even touches on their economic situation. Knowing Jesus has that knowledge about our lives should give us comfort. He is the God of the mountain and the valley. Jesus knows when we are walking through hard times. Jesus not only knows what we are going through, but he knows what is coming. We see that in Revelation 2:10. He also encourages us to "not *be afraid*" and "be *faithful*" because if you do, you will get the crown of life. God is outside of time. So, we know he is with us and will wait for us when we take our first step into eternity.

The letter to the church at Pergamum shows us the third thing that Jesus knows about us. Jesus tells them he knows where they are and if they live for him. The same is true for us. Jesus knows when you live in a place that is not living for him. He also knows if we are faithful to him in that environment. This encouragement to the church also shows us we must guard our ways to remain loyal to him in hostile environments. We put our faith in a God who is above everything and knows everything. Isaiah 40:26 tells us that God knows all the stars by name, and by his power, not one is missing. How much more does he love you than the stars? This truth should be a place of refuge for you. No matter what you face, God sees you and knows the struggle. Remember, he has never failed, so trust him.

Jesus tells us the next thing he knows in his letter to the church of Thyatira. Jesus tells them he knows their deeds and service. Jesus again shows us that he knows our what and, more importantly, the why behind the what. What is different between this letter to Thyatira and the letter to Ephesus is that Jesus talks about their effort. At the end of verse 19 in chapter two, Jesus tells them he knows they are doing more now than they were before. That leads me to ask if Jesus could say that about us. As we grow in our Faith, are we serving more now than we were at the beginning? While we may not actively deny Jesus with our actions, are we acknowledging him with our service? Or are we putting things before him and trusting others to do the work? Remember, Jesus wants you to be a part of the most extraordinary story in the world—the story of his goodness and mercy for saving us from sin.

The fifth thing we see that Jesus knows about us is the letter to the church at Sardis. He tells them that he knows their reputation. He says the church has a reputation for being alive, but it is dead. I have used a quote from John Wooden for years to illustrate this to my students. He said, "Be more concerned with your character than your reputation." Character is who you are, while reputation is who people say you are. So, ask yourself, am I truly alive in Christ? Or would Jesus say that people say you are a good person and do good things, but you are spiritually dead? Remember, reputation does not get you into heaven. So, we must be concerned with our character and whether we are alive and living for Jesus.

The sixth thing Jesus knows comes from the letter to the church in Philadelphia. In that letter, Jesus tells the church he knows they are tired and weak. He also knows when we stand for him in that state of exhaustion. I think back on my own life and realize how my actions denied Jesus when I was emotionally or physically tired. These are times when we must rely on something other than our strength. We must rely on God's strength. He is the God who opens doors nobody can open and shuts doors that no one can. God knows when you are weak, but he is always strong. He does not grow tired or weary and always works for our good even when we are not.

The final thing we see that Jesus knows about us comes from the letter to the church at Laodicea. Jesus knows the temperature of our hearts. He also knows if we are helpful. Jesus tells them in Revelation 3:15, *"I know your deeds, that you are neither cold nor hot. I wish you were either one or the other!" (NIV)*. It is essential to understand that Jesus is not telling them he wishes they were good or bad. He wants us to be beneficial to him. Think about it as hot and cold water. They both have different purposes that are helpful to us. Lukewarm water, however, is not practical for anyone. So, we must ask ourselves, are we content with our relationship with God? Or, out of our love for him, do we have the desire to know him more? God can use anyone or anything, but are we preparing ourselves to be more helpful by growing in him? Would you want the basketball in your hands or Michael Jordan in his prime hands at the end of a game? You and Michael both have a chance to make a game-winning basket. The smart choice would be to put the ball in MJ's hands because he had practiced more to be ready for that moment. Are we prepping ourselves for the moments God has for us? Or are we lukewarm and spiritually stagnant?

Some of the things we have looked at from the letters to these churches can encourage us. In comparison, other things can serve as reminders to us. Like the alarms in school that cause us to focus on the steps we need to take to stay safe, these spiritual alarms can get us to divert our focus back to the main thing. If we keep the main thing the main thing, then we are centering our life around Jesus. The worst thing you could do in any situation is ignore an alarm.

We also see that God is actively engaged in the reality of our life. Look at what Jesus says to Nathanael in John 1:48: *"How do you know me?" Nathanael asked. Jesus answered, "I saw you while you were still under the fig tree before Philip called you." (NIV)*. Before we even came to follow him, he knew us. So don't beat yourself up about your past but find peace knowing God knows all you have done and still calls you to follow him. The savior who opened the eyes of the blind wants you.

Seven Things Jesus Has Against Us & Warning for His Followers

Our first warning from Jesus comes from his letter to Ephesus. He tells them that he knows they have forsaken their first love. Now, you may be asking what that means. *The Expiosters Bible Commentary (Abridged Edition) (2004)* gives us two options. It could be that They had moved away from the love they had for others when they first came to Christ. It could also mean they still love each other, but not in the same way they did before. Whatever the case, it can serve as a warning to ensure our love for Jesus has not dwindled. We can do that by going hard after him every day. The best way to do that is to preach the gospel to yourself daily. Tell yourself that you were dead in your sins, but now you are alive in Christ. When we do that, our love for others has no choice but to grow. Sometimes, that's hard because people can be challenging themselves to love. If we are honest with ourselves, we have likely been a challenge for others to love at some point. Yet, no matter how difficult we were, God's love for us never dwindled.

Our second warning can be found in the letter to Smyrna. There, Jesus warns the people not to fall away in the face of suffering. One of my college best friends always told me, "In life, you are either going into a storm or coming out of one." The times we are in the storm or "suffering" can remind us of what's essential in life. Jesus also told the church at Smyrna, *"Do not be afraid."* While most people would leave it at that, Jesus takes it deeper and tells us why we should not be scared. At the end of Revelation 2:10, he tells us he will be there at the end to give us the victor's crown. We can easily fall away when we are scared the outcome of our situation won't be good. When we are in Jesus, we know how this story ends by worshiping him forever in victory.

Warning number three comes from the letter to the church Pergamum. There, Jesus tells his church not to lead people astray and into sin. We must guard against false teaching and teachers. Satan loves to use deception to get us to fall away from God. We see that in Genesis 3:1 when he asked Eve, *"Did God really say not to eat from any tree in the garden?"* There was no bait and switch, or evil magic trick used by Satan. It was just doubt about the character of God inserted into the life of Adam and Eve. It's wild to think that anyone could believe that God could not be trusted, but that is what happens to us when we believe things of this world will be better for us than the things of God. If we know Satan's tactics, we can learn how to stop his advancement. So, we must be able to answer the question when the enemy asks us, "Did God say?" with God's word. Jesus used the same approach in the wilderness when Satan tempted him. So, spend time in God's word and hide it in your heart. That way, you can be faithful to him and avoid denial.

The fourth warning comes from the letter Jesus writes to the church at Thyatira. There, Jesus warns them not to tolerate false prophets. Here again is another example of Jesus telling us why. In Revelation 2:20, Jesus says, *"by her teaching, she misleads my servants into sexual immorality and the eating of food sacrificed to idols" (NIV).* False prophets and teachers will tell you things that sound good, but they will take you places you don't want to go. Jesus pulled you out of the pit of shame and guilt; don't let people lead you back to that place. Keeping it real in the streets is about following the good shepherd (Jesus). Shepherds don't lead their sheep into danger. They take them to green pastures or beside still waters. So why follow someone who would lead you to desolate places? If they lead you to danger, they do not have your best interest at heart.

Warning number five comes from the letter to the church in Sardis. Here in Revelation chapter three, Jesus gives a 2-part warning. The first warning is to wake up. This is like when your parents tell you to wake up, so you do not miss school. The same thing occurs in Revelation 3:2. Jesus says, don't miss this opportunity. We only have a short time to follow him. There is a shelf life to the invitation from the savior. Jesus tells them he is coming like a thief in the night. So, we have no idea when our last chance to put our faith in him is. So, we must have a sense of urgency for ourselves and the world.

The second warning found in this letter is to repent. To radically change your heart and turn back to God. Both of these actions go together. You missed the point if you woke up and realized your need for Jesus but didn't repent. It is like hearing the alarm go off but hitting the snooze button. That behavior of ignoring the alarm will not get you to the desired destination.

Our sixth warning takes us back to the letter to the church in Philadelphia. This letter is another example of Jesus giving the command and the reason for the command. Jesus never answers our question of why, with the answer, "because I said so." As a parent and teacher, I have often responded to that question from my kids and students with that response. Here, Jesus says hold on to what you have (the gospel message) because I am coming soon. There is a time clock in this world, and one day, Jesus will return to set everything right. You want to ensure you stand on the right side of judgment when that day comes.

The last thing that Jesus has against us comes from his letter to the church at Laodicea. Here, Jesus says in Revelation chapter 3:17, *"You say, 'I am rich; I have acquired wealth and do not need a thing.' But you do not realize that you are wretched, pitiful, poor, blind and naked. (NIV)"* That is strong language from our savior. Imagine thinking you have it all together when, in reality, your life is the exact opposite. We can be secure or well off by worldly standards but be in spiritual poverty. Look how Jesus explains how to be spiritually rich in Revelation 3:18: *"I counsel you to buy from me gold refined in the fire, so you can become rich; and white clothes to wear, so you can cover your shameful nakedness; and salve to put on your eyes, so you can see. (NIV)"*. True riches are only from God. Our question to ask ourselves is, are we walking around spiritually poor? Are we looking to God for our riches and clothes to cover our shame and guilt? If we look for other things to provide for our needs and to give us security, then we are setting ourselves up for failure. The things of this world will not last, but the things of God are eternal.

Knock Knock

At the end of Revelation chapter 3, in verse 20, Jesus says, *"Here I am! I stand at the door and knock. If anyone hears my voice and opens the door. I will come in and eat with that person and they with me. (NIV)"*. We have access to that same invitation today. Being different from the inside out is the key to keeping it real in the streets. We are different when we are in Christ, and he is in us. Look what Romans 8:1 tells us: *"Therefore, there is now no condemnation for those who are in Christ Jesus (NIV)."* When you put your faith in Jesus, no matter where you are standing, You are in the love and grace of God.

God will always be with us when we accept Jesus and let him into our lives. Romans 8:38-39 shows us this when Paul writes, *"**38** For I am convinced that neither death nor life, neither angels nor demons, neither the present nor the future, nor any powers, **39** neither height nor depth nor anything else in all creation, will be able to separate us from the love of God that is in Christ Jesus our Lord. (NIV)"*. Process this with me for a second. In life and death, we are in Christ, and he is in us. It also does not matter how high this life takes us up or how low we fall. Our physical, mental, or emotional location does not determine if we are in the love of God. That truth is the foundation that we walk on while following Jesus.

Map Quest

These warnings and encouragement from Jesus that we looked at from Revelation chapters two and three are like directions to a destination. Before smartphones with GPS, if you wanted to go somewhere, you had to look up the directions and print them out. These directions kept you from getting lost. Could you find the way yourself? Yes, but it may take you longer, and you may have to go through some places and down some roads you do not want to go. When we act as the navigator of our lives, we set ourselves up to be humbled. I know from personal experience that trying to make your own way is hard.

Jesus explains this very truth in Matthew 7:13-14 when he says, *"**13** 'Enter through the narrow gate. For wide is the gate, and broad is the road that leads to destruction, and many enter through it. **14** But small is the gate and narrow the road that leads to life, and only a few find it. (NIV)"* So, we must diligently walk the straight and narrow to avoid destruction. Luckily, we have directions from God (The Bible) to help guide us to the right destination. The directions also help us check ourselves to ensure we are on the right path. Show me someone whose bible is falling apart, and I will show you someone who built their life on the rock. When the storms come, they will not be shaken or destroyed. Take some time and dive into God's word. When we make time and space for God, he will fill it.

Class Break

One of the best sounds you can hear in school is the bell ringing. The bell can send you to your next class, or the bell can send you home for the day. This sound can cause joy or dread depending on your next destination. I am sure you have had at least one class; you could not wait for the bell to ring so you could leave. If that happens to be one of my classes, let me start by saying I am sorry. It was never my goal to make you miserable. There was a ninth-grade biology class with 31 freshmen blessed with strong personalities that I might have made share in the misery they caused. However, that group ended up being some of my favorite kids.

As you can see, just like students, teachers have classes that can't wait for the bell to ring. If you caused that for me or another teacher, know we still love you. Look at us now; we made it. I can not speak for my students, but I have learned something from them, and I hope they learned something from me. There is no cap to knowledge, and I am thankful for my students' lessons they have shown me over the years. Sometimes, God speaks through nature, and sometimes through messengers. God used all of you to help me grow in him.

The reasons for wanting to leave that particular class or classes in school can vary. It could be because you did not like the teacher. Or you did not like the subject material. Maybe it was you who did not have any friends in that particular class. It could also be you were looking forward to the next class because you got to see the person you were crushing on. I did not realize it when I was a student, but it is easy to see when kids start crushing on each other. In school, puppy love is a real thing that affects millions around the world each year. Whatever the case for wanting to leave, the bell was a sweet melody in your ear.

Now, the first part of this book may have been hard to get through at some points. The discomfort was necessary to address the problem and issues. It will always be a challenging process anytime you start examining your shortcomings. I hope you have learned the following things. First, God does not want you to live a masquerading life before everyone. God knows the truth of your heart. It's ok not to have it all together. Finding friends with whom you can be open and honest is a blessing from God. Secondly, I hope you see some of the root causes of why we deny Jesus with our actions. Lastly, I pray above anything else that by this point, you have secured your salvation, and that Jesus is your savior and king.

Up Next

The next part of this journey centers around one overarching question. How do I live out my walk with Jesus? I want to dive into and understand Paul's instructions in Philippians 2:12-13 where he says, *"12 Therefore, my dear friends, as you have always obeyed—not only in my presence, but now much more in my absence—continue to work out your salvation with fear and trembling, 13 for it is God who works in you to will and to act in order to fulfill his good purpose. (NIV)"* However, I do not want to give you a bible verse or a bumper sticker advice and leave it for you to figure out alone. Ultimately, when I tell you to keep it real in the streets at the end of this book, I want you to know how God wants you to accomplish that. Instructions are important. That is why they send you a step-by-step guide when you have to assemble something. I hope this next part of the book is like that for you, but the Bible will always be the best guide. Spending time in God's word is where you learn and grow the most. Don't sacrifice time in God's word for other things.

Please understand what I am trying to get across to you. Our works do not earn our salvation. Our salvation and redemption from sin is in and through the life, death, and resurrection of Jesus Christ. We do have a process that we have to work at. Jesus told us in Matthew 16:24 that anyone wanting to follow him must deny themselves and pick up their cross. Both of these things take work. Denial of what we want and pursuing what God wants takes time studying God's word and learning about him. The closer we grow to him, the better we will get at living for him.

A Roman cross weighed somewhere around 165 pounds. Carrying that load was a challenging task. So, it will be when you try to live for Jesus. If you want easy, then don't follow the teachings of Jesus. The path of least resistance is always the easiest. If you want peace, however, there is only one gate to enter through: Jesus. So, if carrying our cross is part of the process, then we must trust the process.

Our first stop in the second half of our journey will explore Jesus's most famous sermon, the Sermon on the Mount. I think the best start is always with Jesus. I have told students and players to "keep the first thing first" for years. I feel like I should take my own advice during this journey. John's gospel tells us this in the first three verses of chapter one when he says, *"In the beginning was the Word, and the Word was with God, and the Word was God. 2 He was with God in the beginning. 3 Through him all things were made; without him nothing was made that has been made."* *(NIV)*. Since everything started with Jesus, it only makes sense to explore his teachings on how to live first.

We will break Jesus's *Sermon on the Mount* into three different sections. Each focus on various aspects of following him. Understanding each part is essential to honoring Jesus with our life. We will look at the account in Matthew, chapters 5-7. While entire books have been written on this sermon, we will break it into three chapters. Context is a big key in understanding scripture. One of the best ways to understand context is to read the scripture as a whole. So, while we will break it down into three chapters, Jesus gave this as one fluid sermon. The Bible is 66 different books, making up one unified story of God's love and grace. Sometimes, it's hard to understand, but it all fits together.

The second thing we will examine is Apostles' letters to different churches and people. These were people like you and me who heard the gospel's good news and trusted in Jesus. Also, like us, they were prone to falling into denial of Jesus by how they were living. It was never about a one-time experience with these people but a lifetime of following Jesus. This part will address some of the issues we will face worldwide.

95 'Brave

I can proudly say that I have never been a bandwagon fan. Loyalty is a fantastic trait to practice but be warned: It comes with pain. I know because I have been an Atlanta Braves fan my entire life. As a Braves fan, I have seen the highest of highs and the lowest of lows. Through it all, I have been doing the chop every year.

When I was little, my grandparents (huge Braves fans) had a VHS copy of the Braves World Series championship in 1995. This gave a behind-the-scenes look at the entire playoff run. One of the things that stood out to me was when David Justice called out to the fans for not being behind the team as much as they had in the past. This upset the Braves fan base. In the series' next game, David Justice hit a home run, giving the Braves the lead in game six. The announcer said it's okay to talk as long as you can walk the walk.

For the next part of our journey, we should listen to Jesus's words because he could walk the walk. Words and instructions are empty and meaningless if you can't back them up. Jesus walked the walk better than anyone. For us to be able to walk the walk and not just talk the talk about keeping it real in the streets, we must follow Jesus's words with everything we have.

Get to Class

All the different schools I have been to have a few things in common. No matter the location or make-up of the school, when the tardy bell rings for class, there are always students in the hall. The problem is that I have never seen a teacher teach in the hall. So, if students are in the hall, they miss the presented content. The same is true for us. We miss the point if we are just in the building but not in class learning. Jesus's teachings were not designed for people to hear and then move on from. The same is true for us. If we go to church and listen to the sermon but don't try to apply it to our lives, why are we going? Or if we read our bible just to say we read it instead of sitting in the word and letting it change our hearts. This journey is not about checking boxes. It is about living out the change in your heart.

I think sometimes we live our Christian lives in the hallway after the bell rings. I mean that we give our life to Jesus but never move on from that point. I would bet we all have had that same feeling when we read a Bible passage and think, what does that even mean? If you have, just know you are not alone. We even see this behavior from the guys who got to hear it straight from the mouth of Jesus. Look at Mark 4:10: *"When he was alone, the Twelve and the others around him asked him about the parables. (NIV)"* Jesus had just finished teaching parables, and the disciples were lost. They did not understand what they meant. The difference is, they went and asked what it meant. So, we must ask ourselves, how hard are we going after the answers? How much does it mean to us to get it right?

Part of keeping it real in the streets is effort. It will be a big key for the following sections. I aim to give you something other than the Drew Hall plan of how to live for Jesus. People don't want another opinion. They want the truth, and we can handle it! I want to encourage and inspire you to go back to the bible and dive in headfirst. That is where the absolute truth is found. One of the questions I always hear is, "How do I know I am saved?". One of the ways I like to respond is by asking how hard you are trying to get it right and why you want to get it right. Are you trying to get it right to be ok with God? Or are you trying to get it right because your faith in Jesus made you right with God, and you want to live for him? Keeping it real in the streets does not come from fear of punishment. It comes from a love for a faithful, merciful savior.

Students and teachers always look forward to Christmas and spring break because they serve as a reset. They get away from the grind of the school year and just take a breath or catch up on sleep. I hope this short break has done that for you. Now, let's return to our journey to figure out how to keep it real in the streets.

Chapter 7

Code of Conduct

*Psalm 19:7-8 " 7The law of the LORD is perfect, refreshing
the soul.
The statutes of the LORD are trustworthy, making wise the simple. 8
The precepts of the LORD are right, giving joy to the heart. The
commands of the LORD are radiant, giving light to the eyes.*

Honestly, middle school is a wild time in anyone's life.
Hallways and classrooms are full of teenagers and pre-teens
full of raging hormones. This, plus the fact that the human
brain does not mature until the mid-to-late twenties, is a possible
reason why kids do stupid things in middle school. On top of that, kids
are looking to find their identity in anything and everything. The
hormones and the underdeveloped brain create an environment that
can easily lead to destructive behavior. That behavior could be avoided
if kids think about the consequences of their actions, but how many
kids do you know think like that?

School systems around the country use a code of conduct to help
show students how they expect them to behave when they are a
member of that school's student body. When students' behavior gets
outside of the lines that the code of conduct sets, students will face the
appropriate discipline. This discipline can range from writing sentences
to being placed in an alternative school setting. The punishment
depends on the egregiousness of the crime. Back in the day, when

people walked fifteen miles uphill both ways to school in the snow, they had capital punishment in schools. This punishment required introducing a wooden paddle to a student's behind. I'll never forget my first and only paddling. It was in my freshman year, and my punishment got carried out in front of an audience, the entire girls' basketball team. I still appreciate that "character-building" my coach was trying to show me.

Most of the punishments handed out to students during my time in middle school consisted of one of the longest sentences I had ever seen in my entire life. It was a direct excerpt from the school's code of conduct. Teachers would pass that bad boy out freely to any worthy student. You knew you were in trouble at school too much when you had that sentence memorized. I did not have it memorized, but some buddies of mine still know it by heart to this day. The point of the code of conduct was not to get students in trouble but rather to give them guard rails to keep them out of trouble.

Codes of conduct do not just end at school. Businesses, the military, and even the federal government have policies and procedures for how they expect employees to conduct themselves. The military uses the Uniform Code Of Military Justice as its guidelines for policy and behavior. In that document, they even have a catch-all for people in command. When an officer acts in a way that dishonors or disgraces the uniform, they call it conduct unbecoming of an officer. The reason is that they represent something more than themselves. The same is true for us. We represent something bigger than ourselves, no matter the setting.

Authority

The Sermon on the Mount, found in the Gospel of Matthew, covers three chapters and over one hundred verses of scripture. The first part of the sermon (Matthew chapter 5) is the context we will examine for this chapter. There, Jesus explains the map of how to find him in a world broken by sin. It also lays out what he wanted his followers to be and do.

It is important to note that Jesus is giving this sermon on the mountainside. The setting is an essential detail by Matthew. One of Matthew's goals when writing his account of Jesus' life was to show that Jesus was the greater Moses. Moses led the people out of bondage, and he was the one who met with God to find out how the people of God were to conduct themselves. Here, we see Jesus doing the same thing, explaining how the people of God are to conduct themselves. The difference is that Jesus did not have to get instructions from God because he was God in the flesh. Jesus held all authority. One thing you can see in Matthew's entire gospel account is that he was trying to show that Jesus is the long-awaited Messiah.

Instructions are more helpful when they come from someone with authority. The general person does not get to make the policies and procedures in schools and the workplace. They come from the one who is in charge. When you think the person giving you the instructions is just as confused as you, you have difficulty accepting and following them. It is easier to follow instructions and procedures when they come from the one in charge because the one in charge has authority over you. Here, we find Jesus taking that place of authority on the mountainside.

Jesus is the King of Kings. Don't get it twisted; there is no authority higher than him. When we ask him to be our Lord and Savior, we give him that authoritative position. You may have heard it stated like this; does Jesus sit on the throne of your life? If we answer yes, that should impact how we approach and listen to his teaching. It must become more than just a suggestion or moral education. Like the code of conduct in school, there are consequences when you live your life outside the guidelines of God. No matter how much you think it will help you, living outside the guidelines God set for us will only lead to emptiness and disappointment.

Manifesto

Any great leader will have a document or speech that explains what they want to do and how they want to do it. The first part of Jesus's sermon accomplished this goal. Jesus' ministry was still very new, but he was gaining traction. People had heard about the miracles, so they came to see what this guy from Nazareth was all about. We know that Jesus came to accomplish something more significant than what they thought the messiah was coming to do. Jesus needed to address why he was here to the people. While they thought the messiah was coming as a great military leader, in Matthew 20:28, Jesus tells us his purpose was actually the opposite of that: *"Just as the Son of Man did not come to be served, but to serve, and to give his life as a ransom for many."* Generals and Admirals don't go to the front lines to engage the enemy alone. That is not a good strategic plan for winning a war. That is the craziness and beauty of the gospel. The king stepped in to fight our battle.

This sermon explains to those people what his kingdom looks like and how to find it. Jesus also discusses how his followers and members of the kingdom of heaven fit into this world. More importantly, he covers who deserves to be in the kingdom of heaven. The observance of the law was significant in Jewish culture, so much so that people were constantly focused on what they could or could not do. Jesus then finishes the first third of his sermon by showing what it looks like to follow the law.

I will say that knowing the context of the scripture will help us to understand our journey. So, knowing the context of this sermon from Jesus will help us understand it. The first thing to know is who Jesus is talking to directly. Yes, this has implications for us, but the audience who heard this teaching was made up mostly of Jewish people. The ones who had been waiting for the messiah to liberate them from their oppression. While they thought the messiah would save them from Rome, Jesus had other plans. He came to save the world from sin. Knowing his purpose helps us unlock how we view Jesus and his teaching.

We must ask ourselves, are these the words of a madman or the messiah? Adolph Hitler's manifesto was the words of a madman full of hate. If we look at Jesus as a madman, there is no reason to apply his teaching. If we see Jesus as the Messiah, we must follow his teachings with everything we have. Looking at Jesus's most famous sermon as the words of our savior and king will help us understand them and how we should respond.

Kingdom Roadmap

Most people don't look at a map for pleasure. If people are looking at a map, there is a purpose behind the observation. They are trying to find out where they are or how to get where they want to go. The "Beatitudes" in Jesus's sermon accomplish both of these things. First, there are ways to find Jesus and his followers worldwide. Secondly, they also operate as landmarks to help you to realize where you are. You can't know where you need to go until you know where you are. Understanding these two things is vital for the first part of our journey into Jesus' teaching. I can think of no better place to start finding answers to our question of how we live for Jesus.

The following verses of scripture make up "The Beatitudes." These verses come from Matthew 5:3-12 "*3 "Blessed are the poor in spirit, for theirs is the kingdom of heaven. 4 Blessed are those who mourn, for they will be comforted. 5 Blessed are the meek, for they will inherit the earth. 6 Blessed are those who hunger and thirst for righteousness, for they will be filled. 7 Blessed are the merciful, for they will be shown mercy. 8 Blessed are the pure in heart, for they will see God. 9 Blessed are the peacemakers, for they will be called children of God. 10 Blessed are those who are persecuted because of righteousness, for theirs is the kingdom of heaven.*

11 "Blessed are you when people insult you, persecute you, and falsely say all kinds of evil against you because of me. 12 Rejoice and be glad, because great is your reward in heaven, for in the same way they persecuted the prophets who were before you (NIV)."

The first step is understanding what the word *"blessed"* means. Pastor Ben Stuart said while preaching on this text that the word *"blessed"* referred to the posture of the person, not the actual act itself. This falls in line with Jesus' teachings throughout his ministry on Earth. The religious leaders and people thought it was about what the person does on the outside that makes them "clean." Jesus flipped that form of thinking when he said it's about what's inside the person that makes them good. So, it is not about doing an act to earn a blessing. It is about the posture of your heart and why you are doing those things. So don't think of this as a transaction. Jesus is not saying you will get a blessing if you do these things. Jesus says that if you are these things, you are already blessed. By taking this kind of posture, two things will happen in our lives. The first one is it will draw closer to God. The second is that we will point people to the savior.

#Blessed

As we look at each part of the beatitudes, take some time to ask yourself a few questions. The first question is, does my life have this kind of posture? The second question is, am I pointing people to Jesus? One of the easiest ways to make sure you are living out your answers is to preach the gospel to yourself daily. So often, we focus on telling others, but we need to be reminded of the good news, too. We were lost in sin and separated from God, but we are found and redeemed in the life, death, and resurrection of Jesus Christ.

This is going to be a quick trip through the Beatitudes. Think of it like a flyover from a plane at a sporting event. Being a part of a flyover would be awesome, but you miss much of the game. Please take time to really dig into this teaching from Jesus. There are a lot of books that can help you understand Jesus teaching from this sermon. For now, let's do our flyover of the Beatitudes.

Blessed are the poor in spirit

We are spiritually poor because of our sins. No matter how hard we work or how much money we have, we can not regain our right standing with God. So, in God's economy, we must understand that we are poor because of our sins. When we realize this, that is where the blessing comes in. When we know we are spiritually deficient, then we recognize our need for a savior.

Blessed are those who mourn.

When we realize our spiritual poverty, the question is, do we feel bad about it? This realization that we screwed up should cause you to feel bad. This is the first step of repentance. You see what you did wrong, and you feel bad about it. The feeling of regret or guilt is one of the driving forces for wanting to change. If what you did does not make you feel bad, then why would you want to change? So, we mourn what our sin causes us to feel and the reality of the consequences of sin.

Blessed are the meek

This blessing comes from understanding we can do nothing in our power. Because of that, we fall on God's power. It is in the power of God we find refuge and peace. Paul explains this to us in 2nd Corinthians 12:9 when he says, *"But he said to me, "My grace is sufficient for you, for my power is made perfect in weakness." Therefore, I will boast all the more gladly about my weaknesses, so that Christ's power may rest on me (NIV)."* No matter how physically strong we are, we are spiritually weak. Don't forget that when we have Jesus in us, we have the one who defeated death. So, though we are weak, we have the lion from the tribe of Judah living inside of us. There is no person or thing stronger than him!

Blessed are those who hunger and thirst for righteousness

Do you want your life to be filled with what is good and right? That's an easy question because we all want that. Realizing, though, that the things of this world are not suitable and will never satisfy you is critical to where this blessing is found. Where do we look if things in the world won't satisfy that hunger inside us? We must look to the source of righteousness, and that is Jesus. Then, it becomes a process of feeding that hunger with the things of God. Remember, God and God alone is the only thing that could ever satisfy a person. Therein lies the blessing for wanting and searching for those things. Because it leads you to God, from whom all blessings flow.

Blessed are the merciful.

When we were spiritually in debt to God, he sent Jesus to pay our price. God showed us mercy when we did not deserve it, so we can also show it to others because we know what it is like to have it delivered to us. I encourage you to remember the cross if you struggle to show mercy. We did not deserve it, but Jesus still gave his life to us. That includes all the people you love and all the people you hate.

Blessed are the pure in heart

Are our motives pure? Are we coming to God out of our need for him, or are we looking to get something from him? Some people struggle because they see God as a magic genie who will give us our wishes when we ask him. Alternative motivations will always keep you from being pure at heart. When our motives for approaching God are pure, we will see him. Again, this goes back to looking at the posture of our hearts. A good question is, is it enough if I only had God? If you can answer yes, your heart is likely on the right track.

Blessed are the peacemakers

One of Jesus's titles throughout the Bible is "Prince of Peace." He earned that title by making peace between the people of this world and God. Our sins made us enemies of God, but Jesus' life, death, and resurrection made us children of God. Kids will look and act like their parents. So, if we look like Jesus, we should look like peacemakers— not starting conflicts but trying to help Jesus's mission of telling people the good news of the restoration to God. Pointing people to Jesus's love and grace is the best form of de-escalation. Too many people practice stirring the pot. As followers of Jesus, we should practice the opposite.

Blessed are those who are persecuted because of righteousness

We are blessed when facing hard things because we live for Jesus. Look at what Jesus says to his disciples in John 15:18-19 *"18 "If the world hates you, keep in mind that it hated me first. 19 If you belonged to the world, it would love you as its own. As it is, you do not belong to the world, but I have*

chosen you out of the world. That is why the world hates you. (NIV)". When we
are not of this world, we are of the kingdom of God. There is no more
immense blessing than getting to be with God forever. Nobody wants
to hang around someone who makes them feel guilty for their choices.
We naturally try to hide from guilt and shame. Don't let people's
rejection overshadow the blessing of living for God. Remember to
make sure you count the cost of following Jesus. If Jesus is not worth
it, you will fall away at the first sign of struggle.

**Blessed are you when people insult you, persecute you, and
falsely say all kinds of evil against you because of me**

The question we have to ask ourselves here is, do we still want to
follow after Jesus, even if it costs us everything? People will look at you
differently, and they may even avoid you. Would you still go even if no
one goes with you? We are blessed when we don't fall away when
following Jesus gets hard. Paul explains some blessings from holding
fast to Jesus even in the face of persecution and suffering. Romans 5:3-
4 *". 3 Not only so, but we also glory in our sufferings, because we know that
suffering produces perseverance; 4 perseverance, character; and character, hope
(NIV)."*

All of the beatitudes work together. When we posture our
hearts correctly, we can see all these things in our lives. This is not a
checklist to work through. Instead, it is a continuous cycle flowing
through the members of God's kingdom. In the same way, water does
not have an ending point in its cycle; the cycle of the lessons of the
Beatitudes should flow through our lives. One leads to the next and
then back to the beginning. We keep living out this posture of our
hearts till we are with Jesus forever in his glory.

Clear Eyes, Full Hearts, Can't Lose

Friday Night Lights was one of the best high school drama
programs on TV. It was about a town in Texas and how much people
cared for the football team. Everyone was focused on winning a state
championship, from the business owners to the mayor. The team's

motto was Clear eyes and full hearts can't lose. We can apply that same thinking to Jesus's teaching. When our eyes are focused and not distracted, we are in a better position to follow Jesus. A heart filled with God's love and mercy can help fulfill the desire to continue carrying your cross.

The next part of the sermon explains the purpose of the members of the kingdom of God. Understanding the primary purpose you are called to in this life helps you focus on what matters. You can accomplish more things when you have that kind of laser focus. Many students struggle because they can't focus on the main thing. Or they don't know what the main thing is. That's the great thing about the bible; it tells you that the main thing will always be God's glory. Those things we achieve for God's glory will fill your heart in a way that the things of this world never could. We find peace knowing that our actions are for something bigger than ourselves. If your life is filled with working and accomplishing things for the kingdom, you can reflect on a well-lived life at the end of your time on this side of heaven. It also sets you up to hear "well done" from Jesus when you meet him face to face.

Jesus called his followers the *"Salt of the earth"* in Matthew 5:13. Salt has many uses. It helps preserve food and adds flavor to food. Salt is also a disinfectant and was used in parts of healing ointments during Jesus's time. As followers of Jesus, all those things are our purpose in the world. To help preserve the world from the moral decay caused by sin. Followers of Jesus add flavor by letting the love and grace of God overflow from our hearts into the world. We also help point people dealing with this world's hurt to Jesus. The early church grew through these three things after Jesus's resurrection and ascension. They lived opposite the way the world around them did and, as a result, were happier than the world around them. The same is true for us when we live as the salt of the earth. It is not just a motto; it's a mission statement of purpose.

Jesus asks an interesting question after calling his followers the salt of the earth. If salt loses its saltiness, how can it be made salty again? It is important to know that salt is a compound of two elements. Pure compounds of salt can not lose their saltiness. However, some salt would be mixed with other minerals during this time. Because it was not a pure compound, it could lose its effectiveness. Once it had lost its effect, it was thrown out on the roofs of people's houses. The roofs of houses were places where people would gather and hang out. So, when the salt had lost its effect, it was thrown on the roof, and people would trample over it. As followers of Jesus, we are called to be pure salt. Not salt mixed with things of this world. When we start adding parts of the world to our hearts, we lose our effect on the Earth.

Jesus also gave his followers another title, *"the light of the world."* Understanding that the world is in darkness because of sin is critical. Just like in Genesis, where God separated light from darkness during creation, he did the same thing by sending his son into the world. Jesus even calls himself the light of the world in John 8:12: *"**When** Jesus spoke again to the people, he said, "I am the light of the world. Whoever follows me will never walk in darkness, but will have the light of life (NIV)."* We are the light of the world because we have the light of the world (Jesus) inside us. Light can be a symbol of hope for people. Johnny Cash talked about how, when he was at his lowest point, he crawled into a cave to die. The light coming through the darkness led him out. He went from living for himself in darkness to walking in the light and living for God. He even went on crusades with Billy Graham to spread the gospel.

Light is used by people to drive out the darkness. That's why you don't put lamps under tables. You put them on the table to give light to the entire room. Followers of Jesus function the same way. We should not hide Christianity from the world. We must understand that, as followers of Jesus, we are like a city on a hill. People from all around could see the light from an elevated town. We should live out our Christianity like that so we can draw the world out of darkness into the marvelous light of Jesus.

Jesus was the ultimate personification of the salt of the Earth. He is the one who, through his sacrifice, preserves us from ultimate decay. Jesus adds flavor and also heals the hurts of our broken world. We have also seen that Jesus told us that he is the light of the world because the world in darkness has access to the light of life through him. So, the biggest takeaway from this part of Jesus's sermon is simply this: It is in Jesus and through Jesus that we, as his followers, can be the salt of the earth and the light of the world.

Discipline Leads to Freedom

The phrase "discipline leads to freedom" sounds like an oxymoron. Through the discipline of ourselves, we gain the freedom to do what we need to do. Joko Willink has a great book called "Discipline Equals Freedom" where he expands on this line of thinking. We don't think that rules will give us freedom, but they do. That's why Jesus said he came to fulfill the law, not overthrow it. God did not give us the law to get people in trouble. People had been doing that since the beginning. God gave us the law to keep us from trouble.

Jesus spends the second half of Matthew chapter five explaining the law' of God. That's why you see him repeatedly say, "You have heard that it is said," and then he says, "But I tell you." Jesus shows authority in this statement by interpreting the law just like the religious leaders of the day. By doing this, he also takes you straight to the heart of each problem. We often think that because we don't physically do something, we do not sin. So, we must not focus only on our physical acts. It is the listener's heart that must be examined. Out of the heart comes the reasons behind the actions.

What actions and thoughts is Jesus calling us to avoid? Jesus tells us the answer in Matthew5:21-48. It is there we see the heart of what causes murder, adultery, lying, and divorce. Jesus also explains how we are to respond to and treat people who would do evil things to us. Why does he want us to avoid those things? Because Jesus knows the hurt that comes from those actions. If I can help my kids avoid something that will hurt them, I will gladly do it. God did this by sending Jesus to pay our debt and guide us.

By walking us through the law, Jesus also shows us that we cannot do it ourselves. No matter how hard we try, we will fail in one or all of these areas. The beauty of the first part of Jesus' sermon is that it circles back around to the first. Once you see that none of us can keep the law, you realize that you are spiritually poor. That leads you to a need for a savior.

After reading Matthew's account of Jesus' sermon in chapter 5, you should know a few things as followers of Jesus. The first is the road map for finding Jesus and his followers. The second is our purpose for what we should do here on Earth. The third is the law of God, which deals with the heart as much as a person's physical actions. Remember, this teaching comes from one with authority. It is not merely a suggestion.

Chapter 8

Prayer in School

2nd Chronicles 7:14: "If my people, which are called by my name, shall humble themselves, and pray, and seek my face, and turn from their wicked ways; then will I hear from heaven, and will forgive their sin, and will heal their land (NIV)."

Separation of church and state has been an issue in America since the establishment of our country. Religious freedom was a driving force for some pilgrims to come to the New World. Because of this, the idea of the separation of church and state even found its way into the Constitution's First Amendment. The founding fathers did not want another rendition of the Church of England, so they built a "wall" to separate church and political power. This is important to understand because public schools fall under the government umbrella.

In the early parts of American history, prayer was practiced in school. In 1962, the Supreme Court had to decide whether prayer in school was constitutional. Schools are different from other public places because children must be at school. Because of that, the court ruled that having prayer read over the intercom was unconstitutional. Prayer at graduations and sporting events was later called into question. The debate even went into higher education when prayer at college graduation ceremonies was questioned and debated.

I have spent over 30 years in public or higher education. During that time, I have seen the debate on where God fits into public education play out in real time. I remember getting to pray over the PA system at football games. That was one of the caveats they threw in; students could lead prayer at these gatherings. I have also been told as a teacher and coach that I could not pray with or share the bible with the players I was coaching. Some argue that it's right, while others argue it's wrong. This debate is about whether coaches could pray with players played out on the national stage in 2015. Joe Kennedy, a football coach in Washington, was fired for praying with his players after the game. The Supreme Court later ruled that he did have that right, but it was years later.

As society moves further away from God, it will seek to remove God from as much as possible. I have found that eliminating God never helps. Conversely, I have also found that it helps when you insert God into any situation. Being a teacher is partially being a therapist. I have spent more time than I could keep up with over my career listening to students' problems. They don't tell you that will be one of your primary roles in college, but you figure it out quickly once you enter the classroom.

Being a teenager or a preteen is hard. More kids are going through emotional problems than you would think. Now, I will not get into the causes for this, but in my experience, the majority stem from something that happened at home. Where it stems from is different from what I want you to see. You should remember that while students look for answers in a complex world, we Christians have the answers they seek.

I Don't Know Him

One of my biggest regrets as a teacher is how I handled talking about God in my classroom. I knew Jesus was the way, the truth, and the life sense when I was a kid, but I kept it to myself in many situations. I had the answer and the opportunity to share and let the Holy Spirit work, and I missed it. No student ever asked me if I knew

Jesus during those times, but how I tried to help them was like saying I didn't know him.

I know exactly why I kept silent. I was worried about losing my job. I am not trying to make excuses, but that was the honest reason for my response. I had been told I couldn't share Jesus at school, so I kept quiet. I tried to share biblical truth in those moments without saying where it came from. That was the coward's way out. It was a way of saying I tried to witness without boldly proclaiming what I believed in my heart. Honestly, in the end, it was just an excuse and moments of not leaning on God and his faithfulness.

I am not alone in my actions in those types of situations. You may not be a teacher, but you might have danced around sharing Jesus at work or school because you were worried about the ramifications it could cause. It is easy to live for Jesus at church. Living for Jesus outside of church is a different ball game. The good news is what we did in the past does not have to be what we do in the future. I have started handling situations differently and being more honest with my students when I talk to them in that setting. I just let them know it is not from Drew Hall, the teacher, but from Drew Hall, the pastor.

Pharisees

In the second part of the sermon on the mount, Jesus addresses how we approach religious acts of worship. He makes it clear from the beginning that this is not about the show but about the heart of how you do these things. I fear that we act as the Pharisees did in Jesus' day. Jesus multiple times tells the listeners not to be like the hypocrites that only do these things so people can see them. Look at how Jesus starts this part of the sermon in Matthew 6:1: *"Be careful not to practice your righteousness in front of others to be seen by them. If you do, you will have no reward from your Father in heaven (NIV)."* Anytime Jesus tells us to be careful, we should pay attention.

What are we to do when we hear this from Jesus? When you hear the words "be careful," you know you need to lean into and focus on the instructions that are about to follow. You warn people to "be careful" because you don't want something terrible to happen to them. You may remember your mom or dad doing that when you were little. If the stove was on, your parents probably said, "Don't touch it, or it will burn you." Or maybe the lifeguard at the pool was telling you not to run. That is the same thing that Jesus is doing here. Giving us a warning to keep us from the circumstances of that action. Jesus came to give life, not to destroy it.

The interesting thing about the prayer in school debate is that no matter what the government said, they could not stop anyone from praying. They could only prevent people from praying out loud in public. Prayer should be allowed in schools and public gatherings. However, we should not have prayer just to have it. We should have it in schools and gatherings because of the power that prayer has. Loui Giglio said, *"If we could only see what happens when we pray, we would never cease to pray."* These acts of worship we will look at are not about just going through the motions.

Jesus does not give lengthy details about how to do these particular things. He does address what our hearts should be behind the acts of worship. Should we go through these religious practices? Jesus answers that by saying "when you do," not "if you do" spiritual exercises. It really boils down to who you are doing it for. Are you doing it to honor and worship God? Or are you doing it to honor yourself by doing it in front of people? That is precisely what the Pharisees were doing and what we must avoid.

Audience of One

At the heart of Jesus's teachings is who we do these things for. Jesus explains this by how we are to approach giving, prayer, and fasting. In each of his explanations, he tells us to do it for our father in secret, who is unseen. Look at Matthew 6:4,6,18, *"**4** so that your giving may be in secret. Then your Father, who sees what is done in secret, will reward you. **6** But when you pray, go into your room, close the door and pray to your Father, who is unseen. Then your Father, who sees what is done in secret, will reward you. **18** so that it will not be obvious to others that you are fasting, but only to your Father,* *who is unseen; and your Father, who sees what is done in secret, will reward you (NIV)."* All three times, Jesus says to do this act of worship for an audience of one.

Jesus showed us this truth in another part of his ministry. In Matthew 22, we see Jesus teaching the people, and the religious leaders question him. They first asked him about paying taxes to Caesar. This would have been a hot-button topic because Rome heavily taxed the Jewish people. Then, the Sadducees, who do not believe in resurrection, asked him about marriage and the resurrection. After beautifully answering their questions, they asked him one more. It is in this exchange we see who we should do things for. Matthew 22:37-38 gives us the answer when Jesus answered the question of the greatest commandment. " ***37*** *Jesus replied: "Love the Lord your God with all your heart and with all your soul and with all your mind.'[c]* ***38*** *This is the first and greatest commandment(NIV)."*

If loving God is the greatest thing we can do, then our acts of worship should be for him, not for the opinions of the people of this world. We must be better about not giving people authority who have yet to earn it. Doing things so others will look at you a certain way will leave you empty and exhausted. We find fulfillment when we do things like prayer, fasting, and giving to honor the one seated above everything. The Bible tells us that Jesus beat death and is now seated high above all authority and dominions of Earth. So, we pray to him because he has all the power and authority! We fast grow closer to him, and we give to honor him because he has given us more than we could ever deserve.

Giving

John Wooden said, "You *can't live a perfect day without doing something for someone who will never be able to repay you."* We know that no one is perfect, but this captures the true heart of giving. If we only give to get something in return, then our actions are not charitable but transactional. Those types of actions are for our benefit. For centuries, people have said they did things in the name of God, but in reality, it was for their own glory. This is why Jesus starts by saying who we should give to.

A person in need means they are lacking in some area. Whether it be food, shelter, or money, they have an issue they can't fix alone. The truth is we are all in need. We have already looked at our spiritual poverty as a result of sin. Yet when we could do nothing for him in return, look at how God freely gave his son for us. We see this truth in Romans 8:32: *"He who did not spare his own Son, but gave him up for us all—how will he not also, along with him, graciously give us all things? (NIV)."* Paul again tells us the importance of helping the poor in Acts 20:35: *"In everything I did, I showed you that by this kind of hard work we must help the weak, remembering the words the Lord Jesus himself said: 'It is more blessed to give than to receive (NIV)."* Jesus not only told us to give to people in need with his words but also showed us an example with his actions.

From these two examples in scripture, we see first that God freely gave to us and secondly tells us it is better to give than receive. As Christians, we know that giving comes with being a Christ follower. Giving should be part of our character if we are to be more like Jesus. If we are honest with ourselves, this can be a real struggle. The Barna Group published an article in 2022 that said only two in five practicing Christians tithe 10% of their annual income. The same article reports that 25% of Christians give nothing financially to the church. This could be attributed to the sense of security our finances give us. The Bible tells us in 1st John 3:17, *"**If** anyone has material possessions and sees a brother or sister in need but has no pity on them, how can the love of God be in that person? (NIV)."* We are to show our love for God in our hearts by giving to the ones in need.

Our reward for giving comes when we get to the other side of heaven and see our savior face to face. Jesus says that if you give so others can see you, you have already received the blessing from that act. If you do it secretly, where only God knows, you will be rewarded in Heaven. We will look at where the rewards are stored in more detail later. Giving boils down to this: We give because God has already given us more than we deserve in Jesus. So, our giving should be to honor him, not ourselves.

Prayer

I had a long conversation about God and prayer with a friend outside her dorm in college. Now, in all honesty, I did want her to come to know Jesus, but my flirtatious personality and thinking she was cute probably played into why I was there. Before you judge me, this was years before I met my wife. One of the things that stuck with me from that night was her response when we talked about prayer. She told me that she believed that prayer was just talking to yourself. Where we act like our own personal therapist. I am sure I did a horrible job explaining prayer that night, but I knew that definition could not be further from the truth.

In a 2004 article, the Billy Graham Evangelical Association defined prayer as " spiritual communication between man and God, a two-way relationship in which man should not only talk to God but also listen to Him." Communication is always vital between two parties. For any relationship to grow, there must be open lines of communication. In the beginning, God initiated communication between man and God. It is not until Genesis 4:26 that we see man starting the communication process. If we want to grow closer to God, we must make prayer a daily part of our lives.

Prayer is a privilege. We only have access to communication with God through the life, death, and resurrection of Jesus Christ. We see this truth in Galatians 3:26: *"So in Christ Jesus you are all children of God through faith (NIV)."* Since we are adopted into the family of God, we can talk to our Heavenly Father as his children. We did not earn it, but because of Jesus, we live in it. If prayer is communication between us and God, why do we worry about other's opinions of our prayers? Many kids have told me over the years that they don't want to pray in front of others because they can't pray well. How "good" we pray does not matter to God. He knows what we need even before we ask. So, the quality of the prayer does not come from how it sounds but from where it comes from.

So, how should we pray if prayer is about something more than the words spoken or the audience who hears it? Jesus covers how we should pray in Matthew 6:9-13. Prayer starts by realizing who we are praying to. Then prayer moves into asking for God's will to be done in our lives. After that, it moves into supplication. Asking God to give us what we need for that day. Confession comes next in Jesus's model prayer. Asking God to forgive us while we forgive others. The prayer ends with asking God to be our shield and protection.

Prayer and forgiveness go hand in hand. God shows us mercy when we don't deserve it. How could we ever ask him to give us mercy when we want to show the same mercy, he showed us? When we realize how much God has given us through his son, we should always strive to talk to him. It is like talking to a spouse. You know they love you, so you want to talk and spend time with you. That should be how we approach praying to God. We see that we should pray about everything in Philippians 4:6 when Paul tells the church at Phillipi, *"Do not be anxious about anything, but in every situation, by prayer and petition, with thanksgiving, present your requests to God (NIV)."* So, as Mark Wahlberg says, "stay prayed up" in every situation.

Fasting

The last act of worship Jesus talks about in his sermon is fasting. Fasting was a common practice among Jewish people. The Old Testament provides examples of public and private fasts. Again, Jesus addresses the heart of religious exercise. Look at the warning he gives in Matthew 6:16: *"When you fast, do not look somber as the hypocrites do, for they disfigure their faces to show others they are fasting. Truly, I tell you, they have received their reward in full (NIV)."* Jesus shows us that fasting was never meant to be a way to flex your religious muscles to other people. No fasting, just like prayer, is about drawing near to God.

Fasting can be a response to something that will happen in the future or is happening right now. We see this in Daniel's life in the Old

Testament. Daniel knew from spending time in God's word that the desolation of Jerusalem would last for seventy years. Look at how Daniel responds to that in chapter Daniel 9:3: *"So I turned to the Lord God and pleaded with him in prayer and petition, in fasting, and in sackcloth and ashes (NIV)."* Don't miss that fasting goes hand in hand with turning to God. All three religious practices are ways for us to respond to God.

This was not the only time Jesus discussed fasting during his Earthly ministry. In Matthew chapter nine, Jesus also talks about fasting again with some of John the Baptist's disciples. They ask Jesus an interesting question in Matthew 9:14: *"Then John's disciples came and asked him, "How is it that we and the Pharisees fast often, but your disciples do not fast?" (NIV)."* The Pharisees and John, the Baptist's disciples, were on opposite sides of the religious aisle then. Both practiced fasting, but Jesus's disciples did not. Jesus responds and says you can't mourn while the bridegroom is with them. We know that Jesus is the groom, and the church is his bride. Right now, we are waiting to be reunited with him. Our life on this side of heaven is our opportunity to worship and draw closer to God by fasting.

New Thing

Jesus's teachings were not to fix the old religious practices but to usher in new ones. We see this in Matthew 9:16-17 *"16: "No one sews a patch of unshrunk cloth on an old garment, for the patch will pull away from the garment, making the tear worse. 17 Neither do people pour new wine into old wineskins. If they do, the skins will burst; the wine will run out and the wineskins will be ruined. No, they pour new wine into new wineskins, and both are preserved (NIV)."* This makes sense because Jesus is all about doing "new" things. For example, making a way when there was no way. Isaiah 43:19 tells us God is doing something new: *"See, I am doing a new thing! Now it springs up; do you not perceive it? I am making a way in the wilderness and streams in the wasteland (NIV)."*

Let me give you some examples of the "new" that Jesus came to do. First, he came to provide us with new life through him. 2nd Corinthians 5:17 tells us that not only has the new comes, but the old is gone. That should be good news for everyone today. When we are in Jesus, and he is in us, our old life no longer defines us. Because in our old life, we were dead and enemies of God. In Jesus, we are alive and are no longer enemies with God but adopted sons or daughters of the king.

The second new thing Jesus offers us is a new way of living. Living for ourselves will always lead us to desolate places. Consider the story in John chapter five about the man Jesus healed at the pool. He was paralyzed for the majority of his life. After encountering Jesus, he no longer had to live the old way. The same is true for us! We don't have to return to how we lived before meeting Jesus. We can live a new life because we are different from when we did not know Jesus. We are restored and made whole.

God wants to do something new in your life. We must ask ourselves whether we want the "new" thing for our lives. The unknown of what God wants to do in your life can be scary. Please, let me encourage you with some simple truth if that's you today. Your life may look like a wasteland, but God wants to restore it. But it is not just a dream; it is a reality. God is the one who spoke the universe into being. God is the one who made a way by parting a sea when there was no way. God is the one who lets a shepherd defeat a giant. God is good at making something beautiful out of something completely broken.

Only One Can Occupy The Throne

The throne of a king is typically a one-seater. It usually ends badly when more people start trying to call the shots. The same is true for our lives. When two or more things are trying to occupy the throne of our hearts, our lives will usually be a mess. Jesus expresses this very thought in Matthew 6:24: *"No one can serve two masters. Either you will hate the one and love the other, or you will be devoted to the one and despise the other. You cannot serve both God and money (NIV)."*

So, what kingdom are you storing your treasure in? If Jesus is the king of your heart, then your focus should be on storing things in his kingdom that will never end. If something else sits on the throne of your life, then you will store your treasure on earth. The problem with this path is that that treasure will pass away. Jesus told us that in Matthew 24:35, any structure's foundation is a key component. The same is true for us; we must build our lives on things that won't pass away.

Worry should not be one of our default settings when our lives are built on the proper foundation. Material things and titles can cause us to worry. At the end of Matthew 6, Jesus tells us not to run after these things like the pagans did. So, how do we ensure we build our lives on the firm foundation of Jesus Christ? We follow Matthew 6:33: *"**But** seek first his kingdom and his righteousness, and all these things will be given to you as well (NIV)."* So, make sure Jesus is on the throne of your heart daily, and seek him in all you do. Because he is on the throne and deserves all glory, honor, and praise, we keep it real in the streets by praying, fasting, and giving.

Chapter 9

Focus

*1st Peter 1:13: "**Therefore**, with minds that are alert and fully sober, set your hope on the grace to be brought to you when Jesus Christ is revealed at his coming (NIV)."*

Staying focused on the task at hand can be challenging for some. The problem with losing focus is not that your attention went elsewhere but that you needed to be zoned in on what was right in front of you. As our focus shifts, so do our priorities. When we focus on the task at hand, we usually succeed in completing it. Failure to focus on a given task almost always leads to problems. Think about when daydreaming helped you accomplish what you were working on.

If losing focus on a task describes you, then know you are not alone. The Centers For Disease Control (CDC) reports that 9.8 % of kids ages 3-17 have attention deficit hyperactive disorder (ADHD). They also report that this number has increased over time. The symptoms of ADHD can also persist into adulthood. Just because you struggle does not mean you can't do it. It may just require more work than it does others. Any type of disorder can either be an obstacle or an opportunity. It just depends on how you look at it.

Lack of focus during communication can also be problematic. I always have a lot of things rolling around in my head. Most of the time, it's an idea for a sermon or working out a sermon. It could also be who transfers in or out of Alabam and who the Braves are trading for. Just because you care about it does not mean it is productive in the moment. All of these have caused me to have what my wife describes as selective hearing. That creates an issue when she is trying to communicate with me.

The last part of Jesus's sermon on the Mount helps us dial in our focus on what is really important. In this part of the sermon, Jesus covers a wide array of topics, such as judging others, the golden rule, the gate to the kingdom, true and false teachers, and how to respond to his teaching. We must understand that Jesus is showing us that there is a right way to respond to his words. If we want to keep it real in the streets, we must focus on each of these the way Jesus wants us to.

Don't Judge Does Not Mean Accept Everything

I love the first part of Matthew 7. It shows Jesus's sense of humor and how he used it to teach people. Most of the time, if we see pictures or artwork of Jesus, he looks too serious. Jesus was a real person. I don't believe that he was serious all the time. Remember, Jesus said we are the salt of the earth. It would be safe to assume that Jesus had a great personality. Don't forget that our savior is a real person who went through struggles just like we did.

Jesus tells us not to judge others and gives us examples of what that looks like. We see this in John chapter eight when the Jewish leaders brought him a woman who was caught in adultery. The scribes and the Pharisees brought her to try to trap Jesus. They tell him the law of Moses is to stone this woman for her sins. Then they ask him what he says they should do with her. The exchange between Jesus and the religious leaders is where we learn how we should handle the sins of others. John 8:7: "**When** *they kept on questioning him, he straightened up and said to them, "Let any one of you who is without sin be the first to throw a stone at her (NIV)."* That took all of them out of the equation. It also takes us out because we know from scripture that all have sinned.

So, how are we to respond to the sins of others? We should respond with love and grace. Jesus shows us this by how he responds to the woman in John 8:10-11 *"10 Jesus straightened up and asked her, "Woman, where are they? Has no one condemned you?"11 "No one, sir," she said. "Then neither do I condemn you," Jesus declared. "Go now and leave your life of sin. (NIV)."* Two things stand out to me about Jesus' response. The first is he does not shame the woman. Where everyone else did, Jesus responded with mercy. The second thing Jesus does is instruct the woman. Jesus did not just fix her situation; he sent her on a path to keep her from further harm.

This is the blueprint for handling sin and the sinner. It is also an example of living out the beatitudes Jesus taught us in the first part of the sermon. We all can show mercy because we all need mercy. We can help people walking through dark times because of sin, and we know what it's like to live in the darkness. If you are unsure how to respond, just love them as Jesus loves you. Remember, just because you love the sinner and show mercy to them does not mean you condone the action. Jesus tells the woman to leave her life of sin. That is the complete opposite of condoning that way of life.

Bully Free Zone

If you walk outside my room into the hall, there is a poster everyone can see. The poster says, "No Bullying Zone." My oldest daughter asked me what that meant one day as we were leaving to go home. As great as the poster is, It does not depict the world that we live in. The National Bullying Prevention Center reports that one out of five students report being bullied, and 40% of them believe the bullying will happen again. One problem is that the bullying does not stop when the student goes home. Dosomething.org reports that 37% of kids between 12 and 17 years old have been bullied online, and of that, 30% have had it happen more than once.

Bullying has a significant impact on students around the world. The National Bullying Prevention Center reports that students who experience bullying are at an increased risk for anxiety, depression, low

94

academic achievement, and dropping out of school. They also report that the reason for the bullying is for things like appearance or ethnicity. Those are things that students can't change. You can imagine the helpless feeling that these students go through when they are bullied for things they have no control over.

As followers of Jesus, we must ensure we avoid bullying by following the golden rule and defending the ones who can't protect themselves. If you are unsure what the golden rule is, look at Matthew 7:12: *"So in everything, do to others what you would have them do to you, for this sums up the Law and the Prophets (NIV)."* There are two things I want to look at in this verse. The first is how we want to be treated. The second is how this sums up the Law and Prophets.

Only some people want to be treated the same as you want to be treated. For example, my wife and I love people, but we show it differently. I grew up in a Baptist church. It is normal for me to hug everyone. While my wife is the opposite. She shows her love for people in different ways. So, what does Jesus mean by doing to others as you would have them do to you? We may differ in how it is shown, but everyone wants to feel loved. We see that God treats us with love by giving us Jesus. People also want to be dignified and valued. Genesis 1:27 tells us that we are all made in the image of the Holy God. Because of whom we were made in the image of, every human has value. Bullying does none of these things.

Also, we must ensure we are standing up for the little guys. In the military, they have a code of leave no man behind. As Christians, we should adopt the same strategy. Don't leave people behind to fight for themselves. I know people must fight their own battles, but that does not mean they must fight alone. Sometimes, fighting for someone can be just supporting that person. Sometimes, it may mean stepping in to protect the ones to beat down to fight back.

The Motto

Love God and love others is a simple way to put it. We should all be like the Samaritan who cared for his neighbor in Jesus's parable found in Luke chapter 10. When we are at our lowest, we want someone to help us. We should look to help others out when they are in the valleys of life. What if they don't deserve it? What if they are a horrible person? Well, the truth is we did not deserve God helping us when we were a slave to sin. Grace and mercy were not based on us but placed on us.

Never forget how defeated we were before Jesus stepped into our story. If you are restored through the resurrection power found in Jesus, you know the importance of not living on the ground. I have told my children and students that when they are upset and find themselves on the floor, they don't belong there. I believe that with 100% of my entire being. We have value and worth because we were made in God's image. If he got me off the floor when I could not get up, then how could I not try to pick others up when they are beaten down. Sometimes, we need to be reminded of that simple but vital truth.

In the same way, we should also show grace and mercy to those around us. They don't have to deserve it or earn it for us to show them these things. Remember, we control how we respond to people and situations. As followers of Jesus, we should respond like Jesus did. Let's break out the W.W.J.D bracelets and love people like Jesus.

True or False

I loved any test that had a true-or-false section. That way, I knew I had a 50% chance of getting the correct answer. I have seen that same excitement in students' eyes over the years when we had a true-or-false section on a test. Towards the end of the sermon, Jesus gives us the true-or-false section of our time on Earth: first, knowing the difference between true or false prophets and then between true and false disciples.

Merriam-Webester defines a prophet as one who utters divinely inspired revelations. Jesus' warning here is for anyone who says they speak for God when they do not. How can we know who is a true or false prophet? Jesus answers that for us in Matthew 7:16, *"By their fruit you will recognize them. Do people pick grapes from thornbushes, or figs from thistles? (NIV)"* Looking at the person's fruit can help us understand whether they are real or fake. This is why Jesus told us in Matthew 10:16, *"Be shrewd as a serpent and innocent as doves (NIV)."* People in the world will not always have your best intentions in mind. Evil is real, and some people will try to use you to do evil things. A call to follow Jesus is not a call to live a gullible life. Stay on guard and watch out for people who will lead you into danger.

How do you know that you are a genuine disciple of Jesus? "Jesus addresses this in the next part of the sermon. Simply put, discipleship is about relationships. In Matthew 7:21, Jesus says that only the one who does the will of God will enter the kingdom of heaven. Works in the name of God will not be enough. You have to have a personal relationship with Jesus. How do you know that you have that? Ask yourself if you are living out the beatitudes Jesus spoke of at the beginning of the sermon. Another way is to look at the fruit of your life. Just like you examine other people, we need to examine our lives. Check out Galatians 5 to learn the difference between the works of the flesh and the fruit of the spirit.

Failing to Plan is Planning to Fail

"Failure to plan is planning to fail" is one of my favorite sayings in my classroom over the years. It simply means if you do not prepare through planning, you are setting yourself up to fail. Having a plant to fall back on when things go wrong is always a good idea. In the military, they call this a contingency plan. The best example I ever heard was from Admiral William McRaven. Admiral McRaven was the commanding officer in charge of the operation to kill or capture Osama Bin Laden. Before the mission, Admiral McRaven had a matrix of whether they should cancel the mission if something happened at specific times. That way, it would take the emotion out of the decision.

Jesus ends his sermon by telling us how not to plan for failure. Jesus uses an example of a man building a house. Putting Jesus's words into practice is like building your home on a rock. If you don't put

Jesus's words into practice, it's like you built your house on the sand. It is essential to know that storms will come during your life. That's why Jesus said when the storms come instead of if the storms come. Both people in the parable hear Jesus's words, but only one acts on them. This should lead us to ask ourselves if we are building our lives on the words of Jesus. Remember, Jesus said his words would never pass away (Matthew 24:35). You can search the world backward and forward. You will never find a better foundation than that.

Jesus's words are not just suggestions from someone who might have the correct answer. They are commands from the one who has complete authority. Just like the ones who heard this sermon from Jesus, this should leave us in amazement. The universe's king cares about us and wants to keep us from destruction. The words of Jesus are a great place to start building a life that keeps it real in the streets.

Chapter 10

Leave Room For The Holy Spirit

1st Thessalonians 4:3-5 *"3 It is God's will that you should be sanctified: that you should avoid sexual immorality; 4 that each of you should learn to control your own body[a] in a way that is holy and honorable, 5 not in passionate lust like the pagans, who do not know God (NIV)."*

Dances are one of the most significant memories from one's time in school. Unless you grew up in a town that outlawed dancing. If that was you, I hope that Kevin Bacon showed up to teach you how to cut footloose. Ask your parents if you need to know who that is or if you don't understand the reference. If you think back, you probably remember getting dressed and going to a decorated gym or lunchroom to bust a move. High school dances were different from junior high school dances. Still, I remember the teachers walking around to keep you from getting "too close" to your dance partner.

I have experienced this event from each side of the spectrum. The first was when I was a middle school student, and teachers told us to leave room for the holy spirit. I did not know how you did that when Junvile played over the speakers, but I did my best to comply. When I became a teacher, I saw the other side of this event. Telling students to leave room for the Holy Spirit was a blast. The first time I had the opportunity was during my first year of teaching. It involved a poorly lit gym and Coach Hall with a tactical flashlight. Kids separate quickly when a spotlight hits them. Needless to say, I was not asked to work anymore dances that year. Later on in my career, Coach Hall became DJ Coach Hall. Instead of using a flashlight, I would use the speakers and the microphone to remind people to keep some space between themselves and their partners.

You need to understand that the holy spirit works like a teacher at a school dance when it comes to your sex life. God is not trying to keep you from something so you can be miserable. God created everything and everyone. So, realize that part of that plan was sex. It is not a forbidden fruit but a gift from God. Just like God gave directions in the Garden of Eden for Adam and Eve's good, he does the same for us. God was not keeping something from them when he told them not to eat the fruit. He was protecting them from the consequences of those actions. The same is true for you. God is not trying to keep you from joy but trying to keep you from pain and heartbreak. Keep that in mind as we look at how followers of Jesus are to approach sex.

True Love Waits

One of my youth group experiences was attending a weekend called "True Love Waits." Over the weekend, we looked at what the Bible says about sex and how to live a pure life. It ended with students signing a card stating they would save themselves for marriage. I realize that many students did something similar during their teenage years. Hopefully, that promise was more than just a random card in your wallet.

I don't bring this up to shame you. If you did not save yourself for marriage or made that promise, then broke it. I encourage you to remember the cross. Our sins (yours and mine) were paid for on the cross. Sins you committed in the past, present sins you are struggling with, and future sins that could happen. When Jesus said "Tetelestai" on the cross, our guilt and shame were over because anyone who looks

100

to the Son for salvation shall be saved. Or simply our debt to God was paid by Jesus. As we look at what the bible says about sex and relationships, remember this chapter is to build you up, not tear you down.

Our plan of attack can be divided into three parts. The first part equips you with what God says about sex. For this, we will look at some of Paul's letters to churches found in the New Testament and other parts of the scripture. It's essential to know the truth from the lies. The second part of this chapter is to encourage you. Whether you have been pursuing purity or trying to pursue purity, there is encouragement for you. The third part we will look at is exaltation. God is worthy of all the glory, honor, and praise we can bring him. How we live our lives is one of the ways we can honor him.

We will also try to tackle some of this generation's big questions and problems regarding love and sex. How does society view love and sex? Is porn dangerous to my life? How does my love life play into my calling from God? My goal is to give you biblical answers to each of these questions. I also want to point to you two resources that influenced me and helped me tackle this subject. The first is "Swipe Right" by Levi Lusko, and the second is "Single, Dating, Engaged, Married" by Ben Stuart. Both of these guys are pastors I look up to. Their approach to these topics can also be a resource and encouragement. I encourage you to check them out.

Squared Away

We live in enemy-occupied territory. The question is not whether you will contact the enemy but how you will engage when contact is made. The military uses the term "squared away" when they are ready and prepared for the job they are about to do. My goal is to make sure you are equipped and squared away when confronting the issues of love, sex, and relationships with what God says about each of them. When we are appropriately equipped, we are in a better position to survive an attack by the enemy. We can also turn our focus from merely surviving to winning the battle. The world will try to influence and persuading you with its view on love, sex, and relationships. So, let's get squared away and mission-ready for when the attack comes.

From the beginning, we were designed for relationships. Our first and most important relationship is between God and us. God also knew it was not good for us to be alone, so he created a person of the opposite sex. Some who like you are human but different. Please don't think you are wrong for wanting a relationship; it's a natural thing, hardwired into us from creation. When approaching relationships, make sure you keep the main thing the main thing. If we look at our relationships with our spouses to fill a gap in our hearts that only God can, we are setting ourselves and our spouses up for failure. When we keep our relationship with God the main thing, we will be better prepared to love our spouses in a way that builds them up instead of tearing them down. The same is true if you are not married. No matter their title, a person can never fill the gap designed by God for God. If we want to love others how God loves us, we must prioritize our relationship with him.

Sex was meant to be part of the bond in the marriage relationship but not the foundation of the relationship. We see this in Genesis 2:24: *"That is why a man leaves his father and mother and is united to his wife, and they become one flesh (NIV)."* The Hebrew word for united in the verse is "dābaq." That means to cling to or to hold fast to. This is done by spending time growing together. Too often in the world today, people skip over that part and go straight to sex. It would be like giving a middle school student a car to drive. Could they drive it? Yes, but are they ready to take on the responsibility of driving a car? I promise you would not want a middle school student driving a vehicle on the open roads. They would hurt themselves or others. Are you prepared for the consequences and responsibility and the commitment that comes when sex is put into the equation? If you are not ready, then you will end up hurting yourself or others.

Love, relationships, and sex together form a beautiful gift from God. It was designed to be enjoyed under proper conditions. Bringing in a relationship with someone only to get to have sex with that person is being in a relationship for the wrong reasons. The same is true for trying to enjoy sex without the love and commitment of a relationship. A few moments of pleasure will lead to a lifetime of hurt. You cling to or hold fast to something you love and care about. This is why God designed us to experience all three things with "the one," not just "another one."

Keep Going

Sometimes, life gets hard. During those times, it's natural to wonder whether I should keep going on the path that you are on. When I look back on my life, I often have those thoughts after I have messed up something. When you make a mess, you have to stop and clean it up. You can walk away from it. You can pretend it never happened. Eventually, you or someone after you will have to clean it up.

Cleaning up messes is never an enjoyable experience. For example, when you clean the bathroom after a stomach virus has gone through your house, some of the remnants from what happened in that room are left behind. These things are unsuitable to discuss with people, and you probably wish you could forget them. If you ever want to use that bathroom again, roll your sleeves and clean it up. That's why I encourage you to address the mess in your life.

I know when we are looking at our choices and decisions regarding our relationships and sexual life can be challenging. This part is not intended to shame you or make you feel guilty. I want to be like the people you see holding up encouraging signs to those running in marathons. Basically, I want to encourage you and tell you to keep going. It does not matter how well you have run your race so far; I want to encourage you to finish well. It is possible to finish the race of your love life well, even if it started poorly.

If thoughts or memories of your past cause guilt and shame, let this be my encouraging sign for you to finish strong. Lamentations 3:22-23 tells us, *"The steadfast love of the Lord never ceases; his mercies never come to an end; they are new every morning; great is your faithfulness (NIV)."* First, this promise from scripture reminds us that God's love is steadfast and never-ending. No matter how bad we screwed up in the past, That does not change who God is. So, since God's love is never-ending and constant, we can live in that love today, no matter our past. Also, God's mercy towards us is new every morning. God does not run out of mercy for us. Because of this, our past does not have to define our future. Through Jesus, those past actions are paid for and forgiven.

So, whether you have run a great race or messed up at every turn, you can finish well—just like the prostitute Rahab did in Joshua chapter two. She used her body to satisfy the desires of men. Because of this, she would not have been a prominent or respected member of society, but God still used her. Maybe you feel that way. That you are too dirty or messed up for God to use. You can't change what you did in the past, but you can make different decisions today. Decisions to honor God and follow what he says, and not the sinful desires of our hearts.

Glory to Glory

Revelation 21:4 says, *"He will wipe every tear from their eyes. There will be no more death or mourning or crying or pain, for the old order of things has passed away (NIV)."* That is what is waiting for us on the other side of heaven. When we are united with Jesus, all the bad will pass away, and what is left will glorify him forever and ever. That is a day that followers of Jesus should be looking forward to. Make no mistake, Jesus is worth all the praise we can bring to him.

I want you to understand that we do not have to wait until we get to heaven to give God the glory, honor, and praise he deserves. As his followers, we can do that differently on this side of heaven. In the context of this chapter, I want to show you that you can give glory to God by how you live out your relationships and sex life. Look at 1st Thessalonians 4:3-4 *"3 It is God's will that you should be sanctified: that you should avoid sexual immorality; 4 that each of you should learn to control your own body in a way that is holy and honorable (NIV)."* God's will for your life is that you look more like Jesus and less like the world. One of the ways we do that is by avoiding sexual immorality.

How do we honor God through those aspects of our lives? One way to honor and glorify God is to live your love life as he designed. You are not keeping it real in the streets for Jesus if you are jumping from hook up to hook up. The same is true for someone stepping out of the covenant of marriage. Now, please hear me: Your past actions in the area of love and sex do not matter about the decision you can make today. If you have trusted in Jesus and repent of your sins, then those sins are forgiven. It's not about making up for past actions. It's about glorifying God in our lives today because today is all we can control. Yesterday is gone, and tomorrow is not promised. So, stay in your three-foot world today. We do this by pursuing purity and avoiding the culture of the world. When we have self-control over our body's desires, we live in a way that honors God. Glorifying him by how we live is always God's will for our lives.

Big Questions

I want to try to land this plane by looking at some questions you might have about love and sex. Entire books have been written about the subject we have covered during this chapter. If you need help or want to know more, check the books I recommended at the beginning of the chapter from Levi Lusko and Ben Stuart. While the questions are complex, we will look at each with a telescope instead of a microscope. By looking at the question this way, I hope it will take what is blurry and bring it into focus.

Our first question is, how does society view love and sex? This can simply be answered with one word: wrong. Society has viewed them through the wrong lens since the beginning. We see examples in the Bible, from Sodom and Gomorrah to the churches Paul and the apostles wrote to. Even history outside of the bible shows us that people have had messed up views on love and sex. Just look at how royalty used to marry family members. From homosexuality to adultery, the world can lead you astray with its views on love and sex. Knowing that the world wants to lead us astray, we should cling to what God tells us about love and sex. You can not honor God by living out your love and sexual life through the worldview.

Our next question will look at the dangers of porn. You might be asking, is porn dangerous to your life? My answer is yes, it is hazardous to your life and relationships. I saw the dangers of this thorough testimony to our youth group from some fantastic people. For a month, our youth group moved away from hearing me preach and listened to the testimony of our adult volunteers. Both men and women shared about how porn addiction had hurt them and their life with their spouses. The problem is that porn is not hard to find. One out of four searches on the internet are for pornographic material. In our culture today, we love instant and no strings attached.

Instant is not always better. Think about it like this: What would you choose if you had the choice between homemade biscuits made by your grandmother and biscuits from a can? I remember making homemade biscuits with my grandmother at her house. They were always better than the ones pre-made in a can. In your sex life, refrain from settling for easy when you could have something better if you just wait.

The last question is how your love life fits God's calling for my life. We are not mistakes; we are fearfully and wonderfully made. That means God has a plan for all areas of our lives. God designed sex to be enjoyed by a man and a woman in the confines of marriage. Don't let your desire today keep you from the future joy God has for you. I love how Levi Lusko says it in his book Swipe Right: "Now yells louder, but later last forever." Your desires may be screaming at you but remember that what God has for you later will be way better than anything you could have outside his plan. Keeping it real in the streets also includes keeping your sexual life pure.

Chapter 11

Conspiracy Theory

*1st Corinthians 15:17: "**17** And if Christ has not been raised, your faith is futile; you are still in your sins (NIV)."*

I have witnessed a shift during my time as a teacher. When social media became more prevalent and available to younger students, more students began questioning whether what they had been taught was a lie. One of my favorite discussions in class was when a student tried to persuade their classmates and me that the Earth was flat. This led the class down the rabbit hole and discussed other conspiracy theories and their origins.

What was interesting about this was the passion with which the students argued their points. I had a student tell me (who was not even born on 9/11/01) that planes did not fly into the World Trade Centers. I kindly told them that millions of others and I had watched the events live on television. I asked them why they believed these things, and they told me they watched someone say it on social media. It is hard for younger people to understand that just because it is said to a large audience does not make it accurate. The students never cared if the person making the statement had the bona fides to make that statement.

This was not just something I noticed in students; people around the country also noticed the shift in thinking. This led to the CCDH

(Center for Countering Digital Hate) conducting a study on students' beliefs in conspiracy theories. They posted their findings in an article released in August 2023. They found that 60% of students between 13 and 17 believed or agreed with at least four conspiracy theory statements. That number rose to 69% if the students were heavily engaged in social media. The article states that more research is needed, but it also shows the harm social media can have. Belief in conspiracy theories has been a problem for people long before social media.

Corinth

Corinth was a major port city in southern Greece. It had temples to both Roman and Greek gods. The apostle Paul went there on one of his missionary trips and spent a year and a half there proclaiming the gospel of Jesus to the people of Corinth. Paul's first letter to the Corinthians can be divided into two parts. First, Paul addressed one of the significant issues facing the church. Then, he responded with the gospel to show them how to view that issue as believers in the gospel of Jesus.

We can learn many things from Paul's letter to the Corinthians. For this chapter, though, I want to examine the last problem Paul addresses in 1 Corinthians 15. Paul addresses a conspiracy theory that had been around since Jesus's crucifixion. Because of that theory, doubt and misguided teaching had crept into the church at Corinth. In his letter, Paul lays out the pillars of the Christian faith, not just for the people in Corinth but also for us. He wanted them to understand that following Jesus was based on the resurrection.

We must understand that from the time of Jesus' death, conspiracy theories had been spread about his resurrection. Matthew touches on this subject at the end of his gospel account. Matthew 28:11-15 *"11 While the women were on their way, some of the guards went into the city and reported to the chief priests everything that had happened. 12 When the chief priests had met with the elders and devised a plan, they gave the soldiers a large sum of money, 13 telling them, "You are to say, 'His disciples came during the night and stole him away while we were asleep.' 14 If this report gets to the governor, we will* satisfy *him and keep you out of trouble." **15** So the soldiers took the money and did as they were instructed. And this story has been widely circulated among the Jews to this very day (NIV)."* The unbelief in the resurrection of the dead did not start in Corinth, but they had to deal with it. The same is true for us. While we may not start a conspiracy theory about Jesus' resurrection, we must be ready to defend it. Not everyone will believe it. Some will even call you foolish when you talk about Jesus's resurrection. As Christians, part of our purpose on this earth is to tell people Jesus loves them and that he died for them. We also are charged with telling about him defeating death, hell, and the grave because there is no other person worthy enough for us to put our faith in for salvation.

Proof is in the Pudding

It is easy to make a claim about something. What's hard is making people believe you without proof. You could easily disprove me if I said the sky is red. You would have to take everyone outside and tell them to look at the sky. Then, everyone would know that I am wrong. However, if I had told you that fools fall in love because the neuropathways in their brains are not connected properly, it would have been harder to disprove me. Evidence is always required to prove a theory. Even with evidence, you must examine its validity. When it comes to what we believe, we must ensure our belief is not based on circumstantial evidence.

In 1 Corinthians 15, Paul lays out his argument for the resurrection of the dead. Paul does not just give his opinion to the Corinthians; he gives them the pillars of the gospel as his argument. In verse three of chapter fifteen, Paul tells them that the truth he proclaimed to them (the pillars of our faith) is the first and most important thing passed on to them. He also reminds them that they are saved by the gospel message he preached to them. It is on that message that they are taking their stand; the same is true for us. As followers of Jesus, we stand on our belief in the life, death, and resurrection of Jesus.

Eyewitness accounts of an event can quickly disprove a story's narrative. Paul uses this as proof of Jesus Christ's resurrection. First, he said that he appeared to Peter. They knew Peter and heard his firsthand account of Jesus's resurrection. Paul also gives his testimony of Jesus appearing to him. What if they are lying? Paul addresses that by telling them that Jesus appeared to more than five hundred people. Many were still alive at the time of this letter, and the people of Corinth could go and hear it from them. Getting a few people to corroborate a story would be easy, but five hundred people would be impossible. It is not like the disciples erased their memory like Will Smith did in Men in Black. So, all those people telling the same story bring validity to the claim that Jesus was raised from the dead.

Part of being a Christian is believing without seeing. Faith in Jesus's life, death, resurrection, and second coming separate us from the rest of the world. The thing about Jesus's resurrection was that he called his shot like Babe Ruth. He told the disciples what would happen to him, and then it happened just like he said. Because he called his shot on his resurrection, we can believe he is coming back because he told us he would. Our savior is a man of his word.

Useless Faith

Paul argues to the Corinthians that if the resurrection of the dead is not possible, our faith is useless. We see this in 1st Corinthians 15:13-14 *"13 If there is no resurrection of the dead, then not even Christ has been raised. 14 And if Christ has not been raised, our preaching is useless and so is your faith (NIV)."* Paul says that if the message we preach is wrong, we are false witnesses of God. A lot is riding on the resurrection of a carpenter from Nazareth, not just for us but for everyone in the world.

History shows that Jesus of Nazareth was a good moral teacher. We must ask ourselves if we believe he was a good teacher but don't believe he is God, why would we follow his teaching? There are other religious teachers' instructions you could follow. Some would be easier than Christianity. If those religious leaders died and are still in the grave, then we must ask ourselves, why should you listen to them? Death is an enemy that we all face. Death was undefeated until God stepped in. It would only make sense to listen to the one who beat what we could not.

Let's look at some of the founders of different religious ideologies. Buddha, the father of Hinduism, lived, died, and is still dead. Muhammad, the father of Islam, lived, died, and stayed dead. The same is true about Confucius. Don't leave out L Ron Hubbard, the father of Scientology. They both lived, died, and are still dead, just like the others. Egyptian pharaohs, earthly kings, queens, and innovators like Steve Jobs and Walt Disney all lived, died, and are still dead. All of these people had an impact on human history. Some would even be considered a good person. No matter how they lived, they all met the same fate.

Paul says that if there is no resurrection of the dead, then we (followers of Jesus) should be pitied the most. There would be no point in following Jesus' teaching. It could even be considered stupid to tell others to put their faith in someone to save them from their sins who died and is still dead. Remember the conversation Jesus had with Nicodemus in John chapter three. There, Jesus told Nicodemus that whoever believed in the Son of God would have eternal life. That only carries weight if the one who says he is the son of God has eternal life. If Jesus was still dead, then John 3:16 would be empty of any actual value or meaning.

Pillars of Christianity

Pillars are vertical structures made of wood, stone, or metal used as support to hold up the weight of a building. Without the support of the pillars, the building would fall in on itself. Support is essential not only for a building but also for our faith. If no pillars of truth support your faith, then there is a good chance the weight of this world and our sin will make it fall in on itself. Understand that when you believe in Jesus, you are not risking your eternity on something that can't be supported. We will look at the four pillars Paul lays out to the Corinthians in the first part of chapter 15. These four pillars are the truth and the supporting structure of our faith. Building your life on these four truths is part of keeping it real in the street.

We find these pillars of the Christian faith in 1st Corinthians 15:3-6 "*3 For what I received I passed on to you as of first importance: that Christ died for our sins according to the Scriptures, 4 that he was buried, that he was raised on the third day according to the Scriptures, 5 and that he appeared to Cephas,[b] and then to the Twelve. 6 After that, he appeared to more than five hundred of the brothers and sisters at the same time, most of whom are still living, though some have fallen asleep (NIV)."*

#1 Jesus is a real person

The Bible is the primary source of information about Jesus. The claim of Jesus being a Jewish teacher who had followers and was executed in Judea by the Romans is not only supported by the Bible but by other historical documents. You find some of these accounts as early as a few decades after his death. Roman and Jewish historians both mentioned Jesus in their writings. This is important because there is little archeological evidence of Jesus besides the gospels. However, the gospel accounts and Jesus mentioned in other documents prove that Jesus of Nazareth was real. Jesus is the Son of God, but he was born an ordinary man from a place people looked down on. Ordinary people did not usually leave an archaeological trace. The fact that we have information about him from multiple sources shows his importance.

Jesus, being a natural person born of flesh and blood, supports the faith of Christians. If Jesus were not fully human, his living the life we could not be an amazing accomplishment. Because he is fully human, he can relate to our struggles. He knows what it's like to lose a parent and friends. He knows what it's like to be exhausted and hungry. He experienced all of that and still never sinned.

Look at Hebrews 4:14-16 "*14 Therefore, since we have a great high priest who has ascended into heaven,[f] Jesus the Son of God, let us hold firmly to the faith we profess. 15 For we do not have a high priest who is unable to empathize with our weaknesses, but we have one who has been tempted in every way, just as we are—yet he did not sin. 16 Let us then approach God's throne of grace with*

112

confidence, so that we may receive mercy and find grace to help us in our time of need (NIV)." If Jesus was not real, we would not have a high priest interceding for us who understands us. We could also not approach the throne of God with confidence. The good news is he is a real person! So, we don't just have some ordinary person interceding with God for us. We can confidently approach the throne by knowing who is interceding for us!

#2 Jesus really died

Jesus's death is the next pillar of the Christian faith. But Drew, didn't you say that ten out of ten people die? So, how is that holding up our faith if everyone does it? Yes, ten out of ten people die, but it is the reason why Jesus died, and how he died, that makes it a pillar of our faith. It is through his death that our debt is paid. Without his death, we would still be responsible for the debt. No matter how hard we try, it cannot be paid alone. We could never do enough to pay it off.

We see this in Romans 6:23: *"For the wages of sin is death, but the gift of God is eternal life in Christ Jesus our Lord (NIV)."* The price of our sin always has been and always will be death. It is a debt that must be paid. Because we all deserve to die. If we can't pay our debt, the freedom from that debt (eternal life) can only be a gift. God's grace and forgiveness are no longer a gift, if we can earn it. Then, it becomes a wage, and salvation is based on work. Thank God that is not the case for us!

How Jesus died is also important. We are the ones who sinned against God. Because of that, we deserve all the shame that comes with it. But God loved us so much that he sent Jesus to take our place. Jesus is the only one who would be a perfect sacrifice. When Jesus gave his life on the cross, he took on the consequences of our sins. Our guilt and shame were placed on him as he bore our transgressions. We were the ones who should have been humiliated, mocked, and executed for our crimes. That's how much God loves you, though. He died in the way you deserve, so you don't have to.

#3 Jesus rose from the grave

This is the most important of the four pillars we will examine. Jesus's resurrection separates him from the other religious leaders we discussed earlier. From the gospel accounts, we know that Jesus had the power to raise people from the dead. Could he raise himself is the question our eternity hangs on. I am certified and capable of giving CPR to someone who is dying. Helping them go from death back to life. My wife was an emergency room nurse for many years. There, she helped bring people back from clinical death to the land of the living daily. While we can help others, Nobody can revive themselves. When it comes to our own mortality, we are useless on our own.

The miracle of Jesus's resurrection is the ultimate proof that he was not just all talk. Jesus said in John 10:17-18 *"17 The reason my Father loves me is that I lay down my life only to take it up again.18 No one takes it from me, but I lay it down on my own accord. I have the authority to lay it down and the authority to take it up again. This command I received from my Father (NIV)."* Nobody took Jesus's life. He willingly offered it up as the ultimate sacrifice for us. Not even death nor the grave had the power to hold him down.

All of the creation falls under the authority of Jesus. Nature, sickness, demons, time and space, life and death, and anything else in this universe follow the command of Jesus. Because Jesus rose from the grave, you can take what he said and promised to the bank. When you believe in him and confess to him as lord, the Bible says you will be with him forever and ever in his glory. How do I know that? Because the man who has power over the grave said so. The opinions of others don't matter because they have no control over life and death.

#4 People saw Jesus, and people will see him again

When Paul was making his case for the resurrection of Jesus to the Corinthians, he did one of the most important things someone making a claim can do; he mentioned the witnesses. Anytime you make a claim about something, people will always want proof. In college, we used to joke that if it did not end up on Facebook, it did not really happen. It would be hard for Paul to prove that Jesus appeared to him. However,

Paul does not start with his encounter with Jesus; he starts with the others. Then Paul ends his argument by saying that Jesus appeared to over five hundred people, most still living. Witnesses are always crucial in making a claim.

Before Jesus ascended into heaven, he told them that he would return. I can't wait to see that day, but we are not called to sit and wait, staring at the clouds. Since we don't know when Jesus will return, we must live with a sense of urgency to complete his mission. The last command Jesus gave was to go and tell his story. Some missions are only allotted so much time for soldiers to complete in the military. If it goes longer, the men's safety becomes more of an issue. After that time, they have to get off target or off the x. We face a similar situation in our mission. We only have so much time on target before we will have to get off the x. So, we must move with urgency and purpose on this side of heaven.

The first time Jesus came to earth was as a humble servant. When he comes back, it will be as a conquering king. Everyone who believes in him will be made new when he returns. Paul shows us what will happen when the dead are raised in 1st Corinthians 15:42-43: *"42 So it will be with the resurrection of the dead. The body that is sown is perishable, it is raised imperishable; 43 It is sown in dishonor, it is raised in glory; it is sown in weakness, it is raised in power (NIV)."* So, when we see Jesus coming on the clouds, it will be the best day of our life on this side of heaven and the first day of our new life in glory.

Case Closed

It's time for me to make my final argument. Like when a lawyer makes their final argument to a jury, this is my final argument to you. Every day, people get on airplanes to take them from one destination to another. They don't know who made the plane. They don't know if the plane has enough fuel to reach their desired destination. They don't even know the person flying the plane personally, yet they board it and trust they will get to where they want to go.

I have shown you more information and proof of Jesus's life, death, and resurrection than the people who put you on the plane. Even with less information, you get on the plane and trust you will get to where you want to go. The resurrection of Jesus is not a carefully crafted narrative to lead people astray. It is the exclamation mark at the end of the most remarkable story anyone could hear. It is the bow on the best present you could ever receive. As my kids in 2024 would say, no cap detected.

Ladies and gentlemen of the jury, the defense rests its case. You either build your life on the pillars of Christianity or dismiss it as just another conspiracy theory. Whatever you believe on the subject will be the biggest thing that defines your life. For me, the resurrection of Jesus is worth building my life on. What about you?

Chapter 12

3 X 5

Galatians 2:20: *"I have been crucified with Christ, and I no longer live, but Christ lives in me. The life I now live in the body, I live by faith in the Son of God, who loved me and gave himself for me (NIV)."*

The world has changed a lot since I was in high school. For example, when I was sixteen, my parents let me and some of my friends drive to Birmingham, Alabama, to go to a concert by ourselves. This was my first concert and the first time driving that far away from home. So, we head to Oak Mountain Amphitheater to hear John Mayor and Maroon 5. The concert was packed with girls. As a teenage boy, I thought it was awesome. I even questioned why I had not been going to more concerts. The problem was none of them paid me any attention. Looking back, it was that night I decided I needed to learn how to play guitar.

I remember one of John's songs that night talking about seeing the world through one's own eyes and not through the lens of a camera. In 2024, I am unsure if people still print off pictures. I do know that they now get posted on multiple social media platforms. Eksposre.com posted an article by Karl Kinnel that said around 93 million selfies are taken daily. The article also noted that the average person takes over 450 selfies yearly. Not only are people taking and posting pictures of themselves, but they are editing and altering the picture before posting it. The modems.com reports that 71% of people edit their selfies. I did a quick poll of my students and found that to be close to accurate.

Why all the time, energy, and effort put into editing a picture? Because we simply care about what others think of us and how they perceive us. This has become even more prevalent in each new generation. Today, students in my class have grown up with and on social media platforms for most of their short lives. You can't close Pandora's box once it's opened, so to avoid getting lost in the debate about whether we should or shouldn't let kids on those platforms, let's just focus on the issue. As followers of Jesus, we should focus on addressing the questions concerning where our identity comes from. This includes gender, sexuality, race, and other aspects of our lives that shape our identity. So, we must ensure our view on these things matches God's.

Beautiful, Smart, Strong and Brave

While my students lead me to create traditions for my classroom, I have also created traditions for my daughters. Being a girl dad is incredible and utterly frightening at the same time. I do know that God does nothing by mistake. During my college career, doors were open to me to work in women's athletics. I got to be around a lot of amazing women during that period of my life, which helped shape the dad I am today.

Every morning, I look my daughters in the eyes and tell them they are beautiful, smart, strong, and brave. I know they are kids and must deal with bullies and negative talk everyone faces in school. While I can't change the fact that they will face it, I can set the tone for the day for them. I never want them to have to go searching for what defines them. As their dad, it's my job to do that. In this chapter, I want to point you to what your heavenly father says about identity. If you search the world for answers to that question, all you will find is emptiness and disappointment.

I asked my students to write down how the world would describe them while I was writing this chapter. The responses ranged from people thinking they are awesome to people saying they can't dance and everything in between. While not all of the comments were negative, the majority were. This was a small sample size, but it showed me some of the opinions my students think the world has of them. Maybe that is something that you struggle with as well. Listening to the wrong opinions can negatively affect our self-esteem and self-worth. After looking at how God views you and how he views identity, my prayer is that you will realize just how beautiful, smart, strong, and brave you are.

Sparta

In 2006, the movie 300 caused thousands or even millions of men to get serious about weight training. That may be exaggerated, but it affected me, my best friend Cameron, and our Uncle Danny. Some of the best memories I have of Danny were when he made us watch a scene from the movie before we would go into the basement and work out. I want to tell you about one scene in the film as an example of our time exploring identity. King Leonidas asked other people there to fight the Persians about their profession. All of them were something other than a warrior. Then King Leonidas asked his soldiers what their profession was. In unison, they all answered with the same battle cry. King Leonidas's point was that they all had the same identity. By knowing their identity, they knew their purpose. The same can be true for us. When we find our identity, it is easier to understand our purpose.

How would you answer if I asked you who you are? An article from "Act for Youth" states that we have two different types of identities. The first is self-identity, which is when we define ourselves. The second is social identity, where our identity is constructed by others. Both of these can be used to answer our question. However, I want to give you a third option. I am calling this option divine identity.

For followers of Jesus, divine identity is the only one we should be concerned with. Seeing yourself through your divine identity will help you understand your purpose. If you are honest, you have thought about why you were on the earth at one point or another. As we look through the lens of divine identity, we can find the answers to the two most significant questions anyone struggling with identity faces. It lets us know who the creator says we are. It also tells us what the creator made us to do.

Let me give you an example as we look at who God says we are. Imagine if I had used a pottery table to make a bowl to put cereal in for my morning breakfast. The bowl could believe it was a teapot. All the other bowls in the house could tell it was a teapot. At the end of the day, it's not a teapot. It has a specific design for a particular purpose. I want to show you the same is true for us. At the end of the day, we are who God says we are

Who Am I?

To find the answer to our question, we have to go to God to find the truth. It is not just about having an answer; it is about having the correct answer. Like our bowl example, the most critical opinion creation could seek from the creator. I am going to show you five things the bible says you are. I also want you to understand that you are setting yourself up for failure when you look for your identity outside of who God says you are. You will get the same results as if you are trying to buy oceanfront property in Arizona. Just because it sounds nice does not mean it's real.

Maybe you have been trying to define yourself, and honestly, you are just physically, emotionally, and spiritually exhausted. You might even be on the edge of frustration trying to figure out who you are. You may even be just tired of trying to make yourself into something. I know exactly how that feels. For about ten years, I was trying to base my identity on what I did and my success. All I ever got from that was emptiness and hurt. It also cost me opportunities to share Jesus with people because I was focused on myself rather than glorifying God.

I found peace when I started focusing on who God says I am. Look at what Jesus says we will find when we come to him in Matthew 11:28-30 *"28: "Come to me, all you who are weary and burdened, and I will give you rest. 29 Take my yoke upon you and learn from me, for I am gentle and humble in heart, and you will find rest for your souls. 30 For my yoke is easy and my burden is light (NIV).* "Hopefully, by looking at the following things God says we are, we can find peace and rest from the struggles with identity. I also pray that we can truly understand our worth by understanding that you and I are all these things.

Loved

Do you love me? Do you want to be my friend? If you ask God these questions, I can tell you his answer is yes. It is essential to start with love. At the center, all of us long to be loved. I know this to be true because I have seen that desire in students over the years. Most who yearn for it do not receive that love and affection at home, so they search for it in the world. When students know they are loved and cared for, the ceiling on their potential rises. The same is true for us!

It may be hard to believe me, but God is madly in love with you. 1st John 4:16 tells us that God is love. If God is love, then we are his beloved. We know that to be true because of what he gave up to get us back. Later, in 1st John, we learn that we only love him and know what love is because he first loved us. This makes sense because the creation has to learn from the creator. How could we know what love is if we have not been loved first? The first part of our identity is that we are someone who is loved by God.

Masterpiece

The greatest compliment you could give an artist is to call their work a masterpiece. This means that it stands out over everything else. At the beginning of creation, we see that we are God's masterpiece. When God was going through the creation process, he only called creation "very good" after he made us. Man and woman were the finishing touches on God's perfect work of art.

Take a moment and think about how amazing you are, from the complexity of the human eye to the details of our DNA. We were made by the tremendous skill of the master. Just like a work of art is considered a masterpiece, we are priceless. Ephesians 2:10 tells us this truth: *"**For** we are God's handiwork, created in Christ Jesus to do good works,*

121

which God prepared in advance for us to do(NIV)." The second part of our identity is that we are a masterpiece crafted by God.

Son or Daughter

Throughout my career in education, I have tried to treat every student as if they were my own child. That was probably why I was a jerk some days. I just wanted them to do things the right way. It was not until I had children of my own that I understood the difference. While I loved my students, they were not my sons and daughters. The good news for us is that through Jesus, we are adopted into the family of God. We see this in Romans 8:15: *"The Spirit you received does not make you slaves, so that you live in fear again; rather, the Spirit you received brought about your adoption to sonship. And by him we cry, "Abba, Father (NIV)."*

The beauty of being sons and daughters of God is that we can approach God as his children. We get to have a relationship with him that is not formal or business. We get to have a relationship with him that is personal and intimate. Now, I know for some, this may be hard to wrap your head around because your earthly father was not great. Or maybe he was not even around. I think Loui Giglio phrases it best when he says, "God is the not reflection of our earthly father; he is the perfection of our earthly father." The third part of our identity is that we are a child of God when we place our faith in Jesus.

Not Forsaken

One of the hardest things I have had to witness during my career is the aftermath when a parent signs their parental rights away. Watching a kid cry and ask why nobody wants them will tear your heart out. You can see in real-time the issues and wounds something like this causes. This will be something the kid has to work to get through for a long time. I know that the feeling of nobody wanting them can lead people to places they don't want to go. Even though the people in our life may abandon us, our heavenly father does not forsake us.

Merriam-Webster defines forsaken as to renounce or to turn away from entirely. While people may have turned away from us, God does the opposite. Romans 5:8 tells us, *"But God demonstrates his own love for us in this: While we were still sinners, Christ died for us(NIV)."* So, God is not turning away from us; he is running towards us like the father in the prodigal son. Not to shame us but to keep us from shame. Remember that even when we were at our worst, God moved toward us first by sending his only son, Jesus. The fourth part of our identity is that we are not forsaken by God but instead chosen by God.

Not A Mistake

Accidents happen. If you have ever raised or have been around toddlers, you know that it's not if an accident will happen but when it will happen. No matter how you feel, understand that you are not a cosmic accident. It is not a mistake you exist. God is perfect in every way. He always has been, and he always will be. Since you were created by God, there is no possible way that you are a mistake. That includes your existence and everything about you, from your looks to your personality and gifts.

Look at what the Bible says about how God made us. God fashioned us and intimately put us together from conception. God's works are wonderful, and we are the work of God. God knows our minor details, from our most vital attributes to our most significant weaknesses. Our life had a plan from the beginning. It may be hard to believe, but you are exactly how God wanted you to be. Mistakes don't have value. The Bible says in 1st Corinthians 6:20 that we are *"bought at a price."* If something has a price, it has value. So, since we were bought at a price, we know our lives have value. The fifth part of our identity is that we were created purposefully.

Issues of Identity

Understanding our identity and where it comes from can help shape our view of the issues surrounding it. All of these issues will be something that you, your kids, and their kids will have to deal with at some point in their lives. Understanding how we deal with these issues is one of the most significant ways to represent God authentically. For our time together, I want to look at race, gender, human trafficking, and abortion. As Christians, Jesus is the highest authority in our lives. So, we must look at these issues the way he does.

Racism

Racism is a real problem the world has been facing for centuries. You can look back at multiple times in human history and see where one group enslaves and discriminates against another group. No one race is greater than the other. As Christians, we need to understand racism goes against what the Bible teaches. Look at Galatians 3: 28: *"There is neither Jew nor Gentile, neither slave nor free, nor is there male and female, for you are all one in Christ Jesus(NIV)."* Jesus did not tell us to only love those who look like us. He told us to love our neighbor. Your neighbor might look like you or be the complete opposite. How we treat them is not determined by what they look like or where they come from. People of every race were made in the image of God. Everyone should be treated as such.

Gender Identity

What gender you identify as has been a hot-button issue over the last few years. While politicians and leaders have their opinions on gender, as Christians, we must view gender how God does. We see from the beginning that God created two separate genders. While they are different, they are equally important to God. Another side of this is understanding you are fearfully and wonderfully made. God did not make a mistake when you made you a man or a woman. To say you should be something else would mean that God messed up. We know that is not true. Our jobs as Christians are to love people struggling with this issue and point them to the gospel. Remember Psalm 118:8: *"It is better to take refuge in the Lord than to trust in humans (NIV)."* We are all humans, so trust that God made you exactly how you were intended to be made.

Human Trafficking

All life needs to be approached with dignity. Slavery is not a form of dignity but rather a form of oppression. Since its inception, the National Human Trafficking Hotline has identified over eighty thousand cases that involve over one hundred and sixty-four thousand victims. The victims are made up of all ages, races, and genders. A report by the United Nations Office On Drugs And Crime says that 79% of all human trafficking is for sexual exploitation. Every one of those victims is made in the image of God and has dignity and value. As Christians, we must live out Psalm 82:3: *"Defend the weak and the fatherless; uphold the cause of the poor and the oppressed (NIV)."* It is not something we can just look the other way. Part of how we are to act as followers of Jesus is found in Psalm82:3

Abortion

Where do you say that life begins? Your answers lead to how you view the issue of abortion. Over fifty million abortions have occurred since 1973. It is a real problem we will be asked to address as Christians. People will try to defend their choice with various reasons to justify the action. The same is true for abortion. David Platt addressed the problem with the justification of abortion during secret church 22'. David said, "If the unborn is not human, then no justification is needed. If the unborn is human, no justification for abortion is adequate." God can turn things made out of unimaginable evil into something good. While women may not have chosen to have the baby and proceeded to have an abortion, as Christians, we are still called to love and minister to them.

Ice Cream

I remember going to K-Mart with my mom, which was always a blast. If I was good in the store, I increased my chances of talking her into getting me an ice cream from the snack bar. As a kid, I thought seeing all the different types of ice cream in the cooler was awesome. While all the flavors were different, they were also all ice cream at the end of the day. All flavors were designed with a purpose. It would be silly for spearmint to try to be cookies and cream. The same is true for us.

Ralph Waldo Emerson said, "To be yourself in a world constantly trying to make you something else is the greatest accomplishment." Don't be naive; the world will try to make you look more like it. Don't waste your life trying to be something that you are not. When you do that, you will always end up empty and longing for more. Find your joy in being the best version of the loved child of God that you are. I want to leave you with the encouragement of Psalm 16:11: *"You make known to me the path of life; you will fill me with joy in your presence, with eternal pleasures at your right hand(NIV)."* Seek God to find the path for your life, and you will find joy.

End of the Day

The ending is always important. No matter how good the journey was, you would walk away with a sour taste if the ending was a letdown. Let me give you an example, think about a television show or movie that you were really invested in. All that time was spent building to the finish, only to end up disappointed. Like when the Griswolds got to Wally World only to find out the park was closed. If you need help understanding that reference, let me try using something from this century. Look at how you felt at the end of *Game of Thrones, Lost, How I Met Your Mother* or *House*? That is the kind of disappointment I am talking about.

You can experience that same feeling in school. If your last class of the day is terrible, you will probably leave with a bad taste in your mouth. You might have left school feeling defeated if you did poorly on a test or an assignment. Chances are, if you leave defeated, you will return defeated. It would be understandable to ask yourself, why should I go back if it's only going to end in failure? It would also be logical not to want to return. Who really wants to be reminded of their failure anyway?

The same feelings and questions can be present in our walk with Jesus. If all you ever experience with Jesus is guilt and shame, why would you return? You would be more likely to avoid him than move closer to him. You may not think you are a terrible person, but you're not great either. So, you will just stand on the sidelines, believing God could never use anyone like you. Or that he does not want to use you.

I realize that some of the things we have discussed were probably hard to think about. I am sure they brought up old wounds and bad feelings. I can tell you that I struggled with those emotions while writing every chapter. Don't get discouraged if you have felt these feelings during our journey. You are not alone; I want to show you that you are in good company as we end this journey.

Encouragement

As an educator, I have found that everyone needs encouragement. Some of the subject matter we have covered have been hard. The difference between quitting and finishing strong can be an encouraging conversation. When I laid out the outline of this book, I set up our last two chapters to encourage you because, just like Peter, Jesus wants us to finish strong, and he has a plan for your life.

As we end by looking at Jesus's conversation with Peter after his denial, understand that conversation is also for you. You may think, "Jesus does not want to have a conversation with me after what I have done." I am sure Peter felt the same thing. In his lowest moment, God sends Peter an encouraging word. Mark 16:6-7 *"Don't be alarmed," he said. "You are looking for Jesus the Nazarene, who was crucified. He has risen! He is not here. See the place where they laid him.7 But go, tell his disciples and Peter, 'He is going ahead of you into Galilee. There you will see him, just as he told you. (NIV)"*

The encouragement for Peter and for us is the gospel. That God sent his son to die for us, but he did not stay dead. He is alive forever and ever! That risen savior wants you to know that he is alive. More than that, he wants to have a personal meeting with you. All our sin and denial were paid for by him on the cross. Because our sin is paid for, we can restore our relationship with God. That restoration can only begin with a meeting with Jesus. That is good news for everyone who has breath in their lungs. David Platt said it best: "Sin from your past does not dispel hope for your future." That hope is only found in the gospel.

127

Land the Plane

How Jesus interacts with Peter is how he wants to interact with us after we have denied him. Maybe you have not been keeping it real in the streets for Jesus, and coming back to him scares you to death. That fear comes from not knowing how he will respond. When you let people down before, you do not want to repeat the interaction with them afterward. The great thing is that through the story of Peter, we see how Jesus responds to those who deny him. We must swallow pride, overcome fear, and converse with Jesus.

I want you to leave knowing you are loved. I want the same thing for my students, so I tell them I love them before they walk out my door. There are not always rainbows and butterflies in my classroom. Sometimes, I have had to discipline kids, which is never fun. But no matter if it was a great class or if I had to yell and get on to everyone to act like a somewhat normal human being, every kid needed to know they were loved.

The bell will ring soon, our time will be over, and you will return to the real world. You understand the issues with not living out your life with Jesus. You have seen how the bible tells us to live and how to handle different situations. This last part is for you to understand no matter how bad you screwed up; you can leave washed by grace and living for him.

Chapter 13

Awkward Moments

Luke 22:60-62 "60 Peter replied, "Man, I don't know what you're talking about!" Just as he was speaking, the rooster crowed. 61 The Lord turned and looked straight at Peter. Then Peter remembered the word the Lord had spoken to him: "Before the rooster crows today, you will disown me three times." 62 And he went outside and wept bitterly (NIV)."

From adolescence to adulthood, life is full of awkward moments. Some of the uncomfortable moments we have experienced have made us better people. They are the moments you look back on and laugh at in retrospect. In comparison, other awkward moments may have caused you to need to stay in therapy longer. Whatever the outcome, you understand that feeling in the bottom of your stomach when things are uncomfortable.

Most of the time, that awkward feeling was probably because of a breakup in school. Navigating romantic feelings is complicated, no matter how old you are. When you add social media to the mix, things can get turned up another notch. Think about the drama created when someone would change their top friend order on Myspace. If you struggle with that example, ask your parents. Then, when Facebook took over, you always knew when someone was in their feels if they posted a sappy status update. The person did not even have to be in the room for you to feel the awkwardness.

Sometimes, the awkwardness was one-sided. Other times, it could be felt by both people. Then, sometimes, the awkwardness was so intense that everyone in the room could feel it. That only happened when everyone knew what was going on. The chances of everyone knowing are higher in junior high and high school than later in life. I know this because I have watched kids know something was awkward between people in the room and announce why it is uncomfortable to the entire class. I guess Alfred from Batman was right when he said, "Some people just want to watch the world burn."

I have been on both sides of the awkwardness spectrum caused by a breakup. Sometimes, it came even before there was a relationship. When you tell the person you have a crush on your feelings for them, they will tell you thanks but no. I don't know how it was for you, but it was awkward to be around that person after the rejection. That feeling did not hold a candle to when my first serious relationship ended. It was uncomfortable for years when I would see her. I know it was just in my head, but a broken heart can affect your emotions.

In college, I got to be on the other side of the spectrum. While at Gadsden State Community College, I felt led to start a bible study in my house for people on campus. Before you start thinking I was this great guy, let me stop you; I had my faults. I went through a phase where dating was more of a recreational experience and was far from looking for a relationship. I blame my dad for that. He told me after my breakup in high school to just "love the one you're with." Now, that was probably not the most biblical advice, but it did help me not be depressed. Just because something will get you out of the valley does not mean it is good for you. That advice just led to other valleys.

Back to my story, I started talking to/dating a girl who was coming to bible study. I thought she was cool, but I did not know If I liked her enough to get into a relationship. Remember, I was dating for the wrong reasons. One day during bible study, she got up and ran out crying. My mom, the amazing, kind-hearted person she is, told me I needed to go check on her. When I went outside, she told me she could see herself married as a freshman in college. I had to tell her I could not see myself with a girlfriend. She never returned to bible study, but we had some classes together. The awkwardness in those classrooms was thick for a week or two.

One of the key ingredients to awkwardness is hurt. It does not have to be romantically hurt, though. When you let a friend or someone you look up to down, it can be hard to face them. This was what Peter experienced after he denied Jesus. When we mess up like Peter, we can let the awkwardness into our relationship with God. It can be hard to navigate, but I want to show you the awkward feeling is one-sided.

I Am Done

That's it, I am done with love. You probably said this quote or something similar after a breakup. Or, you may have tried to return to how you were before the relationship. It is easy to want to fall back into your old habits and hang out with old friends. Those things are just distractions from the ending of a relationship. It is understandable to want to return to who you were before you were hurt or hurt someone. This is what we find Peter doing in John 21. The problem is that no matter how hard you try to go back, life will always be different.

I want you to understand that sometimes, knowing the truth does not help. You can know that other people are out there for you to date, but the breakup still hurts. The person you hurt can tell you that it's okay. They can even tell you they forgive you, but when you remember how you let them down, the guilt and shame come rushing back. When that happens, you start to doubt the relationship status between you and them. The doubt leads you to act differently around that person. This is the type of situation we find Peter in.

Peter followed Jesus throughout his ministry. He had seen the miracles, but more importantly, he had heard the words of Jesus. Hearing only sometimes equates to understanding, though. Look at Mark 8:31-32: "*31 He then began to teach them that the Son of Man must suffer many things and be rejected by the elders, the chief priests and the teachers of the law and that he must be killed and after three days rise again. 32 He spoke plainly about this, and Peter took him aside and began to rebuke him (NIV)."* Peter heard it plainly from Jesus and still screwed up. More than that, he had been with Jesus more than once after his resurrection. So, he knew he defeated death! Knowing all that truth, Peter still struggled with his denial.

This is why Peter is trying to revert to the old ways in John 21. This happened after they left Jerusalem. When they returned home, the question was, what do we do now while we wait? Jesus appeared to his disciples and disappeared in a way he could only do. After seeing all the events, it would be easy to think about what we should do now while waiting. John 21:3 gives us Peter's answer: *"I'm going out to fish," Simon Peter told them, and they said, "We'll go with you." So they went out and got into the boat, but that night they caught nothing (NIV)."* The Greek word for I'm going is hypagō. Hypagō means going away or "to return." Peter is saying I am leaving and going back to fishing.

Why would Peter do that? He had seen and been with the man he called the Messiah—the man everyone was talking about and who defeated death and the grave. That man had shown himself to Thomas, who did not believe Jesus was alive. Thomas even said he would never believe it unless he saw the places in his hands and the hole in his side with his own eyes. Jesus addressed Thomas's disbelief, yet Peter's denial had not been addressed. We must remember that God works off his own schedule. He did address both situations but at different times. He does the same with us. There can never be resolution or reconciliation without confrontation. Confrontation is hard when you think the relationship is closed.

The Relationship Is Open

Why would you try to bring up the indiscretion if the door to the relationship is closed? There is no point in seeking reconciliation for past events if there is no point in the future. If the door to the relationship is closed, addressing the problem would waste time for everyone involved. Think about it like this: It would be pointless for me to try to work out the issues from a relationship with a girl I used to date. It would be a big waste of time and mess up what I have now with my wife. I believe that when people deny Jesus, they struggle because they think that the relationship between them and God is closed. While I don't have good news about your old romantic relationships, I do have good news concerning your relationship with Jesus.

The relationship between you and Jesus is still open, which is the first takeaway from John 21. Even when Peter tried to return to his old life, his relationship with Jesus was still open. How do I know this to be true? Look at John 21:4: *"Early in the morning, Jesus stood on the shore, but the disciples did not realize it was Jesus (NIV)."* Jesus was the one Peter denied, and he moved toward him first. I want you to understand how important it is to us that God moved first. Think about when Thomas doubted. He did not have to go on some spiritual journey to find Jesus. Jesus stepped into his story and addressed his issues. We see him doing the same for Peter, and he does the same for us. Will you accept him when he steps into your story to work some things out with you?

You don't have to be Sherlock Homes to determine if the relationship is closed. If a person is avoiding you and avoiding answering you when you reach out, chances are that the ship has sailed. If they come to you, there is an excellent chance to restore the relationship. Luckily for us, Jesus knocked on our door. Look at Revelation 3:20: *"**20** Here I am! I stand at the door and knock. If anyone hears my voice and opens the door, I will come in and eat with that person, and they with me (NIV)."* We find Jesus speaking to the church in Laodicea. Even though they were lukewarm in their faith, Jesus still knocked at the door to their heart. He does the same for us no matter what we have done. The relationship is still open! Jesus does not want us in the place or denial took us to.

The last thing we see from John 21 that tells us the relationship is still open is that Jesus had fixed them breakfast. It is important to understand that they had not caught any fish until Jesus had stepped into the story. So, Peter had nothing to bring, but Jesus already had

133

everything he needed. You don't eat breakfast with people you don't like. It's easy to think after we deny Jesus that he does not like us. How Jesus responds to Peter and the church a Laodicea shows us the exact opposite. The interaction Jesus wants with us is intimate.

The Interaction Is Personal

Often, people believe that they can only formally deal with God. To interact with him the same way people interact with a judge in the courtroom. Or the way people act during business meetings. While God deserves all the reverence, we can bring him, we don't have to approach him out of fear. When we accept Jesus, he lives in us, and we live in him. Because of this, we can approach him as a friend. Relationships with friends is a personal relationship.

Look at how Jesus enters himself into Peter's story. In John 21, Jesus recreates two significant moments of Peter's life with Jesus. First, he recreates the miracle of the fish from when he called Peter to follow him. The second way is a minor detail you can quickly pass over. Look at John 21:9: *"When they landed, they saw a fire of burning coals there with fish on it, and some bread (NIV)."* Now, fire is mentioned all throughout the Bible. However, the type of fire mentioned in John 21 is only mentioned in one other place. John 18:18: *"It was cold, and the servants and officials stood around a fire they had made to keep warm. Peter also was standing with them, warming himself (NIV)."* Jesus builds the same kind of fire that Peter denied him around the night of his arrest.

One thing we can learn from this is that Jesus knows us. He knows our highest highs and even our lowest lows. Jesus knows the most significant regret and mistake in Peter's life, yet he still moves towards him. The same is true for us. Jesus knows every aspect of us. Jesus knows every good, bad, and ugly moment of our lives. That piece of truth matters because it shows that none of us are too far gone for God to love and want.

The second way this passage shows us that interaction with Jesus is personal is by how he addresses Peter's major and minor issues. Peter and the others had been fishing all night. It would be safe to say they were probably ready to eat. Peter and the guys did not even have to ask. Jesus already had what they needed. Though minor, the king of kings cared for Peter's needs and provided for them.

While meeting the minor need helped Peter, Jesus still had bigger fish to fry (pun intended). Jesus needed to get his hands on the problem. I heard Ben Stuart explain this by using the story of when he broke his leg. The doctor came in and would have to partially set the bone. To do that, he had to pull and hit the broken leg. Ben said he had to get his hands on the problem. Another way to think about it is if a stranger cuts, you may get them a bandage, but you will probably not put your hand in the wound to stop the bleeding. If the one bleeding is your kid, you will put your hand on it without even thinking. What's the difference between the two? I have a personal relationship with my kid. So, I won't even think twice to put my hands on the wound to help them.

The Importance of #3

Numbers are an essential part of life and can carry significant meaning to a person. Let me give you an example: To you, the number 531 may not hold any significant meaning, but to a recovering addict who has been clean for 531 days, it is one of the most critical numbers in the world. From coaching, I have seen kids pick random numbers for their jerseys. It is random to me, but when it is their mom or dad's number from when they played, it becomes a symbol of pride.

In the Bible, numbers are significant as well. There is a number in John 21 that is important for us. We find it in John 21:14: "***This*** *was now the third time Jesus appeared to his disciples after he was raised from the dead(NIV).*" Why is number three important to us? First, it shows us that interaction with Jesus is not a mistake. This was the third time he had appeared to Peter. One time, interacting with Jesus could be taken as a mistake. Two times, and you think it could be an accident. Three times show it has a purpose. Maybe you think that after your actions of denial, Jesus is not trying to get your attention. Don't write it off as an accident or a mistake if God is speaking to you. If God is trying to get your attention to address something, it is for a reason.

The second reason the number three is essential for us is that it lets us know there is still time. I don't say that to tell you to put off dealing with what's between you and Jesus. I say that to show it took three visits from Jesus before Peter's denial was addressed. So maybe God has been wanting to get his hands on the wounds from denial, and you have put it off. The good news is there is still time to work it out with God.

While there is still time to address the issues with Jesus, understanding now is better than later because we are not promised later. That's why we must have a sense of urgency when dealing with the wound of our denial. If you let the wound fester, your only outcome will be bad. The longer you wait, the worse it is. If you wait too long, it can become too late. The same is true for us. If we wait too long, we will miss how God wanted to use us because we thought our actions placed us on the sidelines.

From Awkward to Awe

I know that you might have been or are currently experiencing awkwardness between you and God due to your mistakes. That may have caused you to feel distant at church. I understand that you might struggle with acting like everything is ok while you are hurting on the inside. It may even hurt how you interact with others at church. It's hard to praise the Lord with arms high and hearts abandoned when you are ashamed. While you may feel like that's where you deserve to be, another option exists.

We need to remember who wants to have a relationship with us. Look at how John describes the risen Jesus in Revelation 1:13-16 *"13 and among the lampstands was someone like a son of man,[d] dressed in a robe reaching down to his feet and with a golden sash around his chest. 14 The hair on his head was white like wool, as white as snow, and his eyes were like blazing fire. 15 His feet were like bronze glowing in a furnace, and his voice was like the sound of rushing waters. 16 In his right hand he held seven stars, and coming out of his mouth was a sharp, double-edged sword. His face was like the sun shining in all its brilliance (NIV)."* It is this same Jesus that is standing and knocking on the door of your heart. The one who wants to get his hands on your wounds and heal you. It is Jesus, in all of his glory, inviting you to be a part of the most remarkable story ever told.

How could Jesus, who is so great and wonderful, ever want to fix me? If that question is the first thing that popped into your head, let me give you the answer. He is good, loving, kind, forgiving, amazing, redeeming, loyal, the way, the truth, the life, alpha and omega, way maker, miracle worker, promise keeper, hope for the hurting, and rest for the weary. That just scratches the surface of how awesome and amazing God is.

When I think about all God has done for me, the only feeling that describes my heart is awe. God would be justified if he decided to wipe me off the face of the Earth. Yet God did the opposite. He gave everything to ensure I had a way to be with him. The same God who gave everything for me still wants me even after I denied him. I don't fully understand it, but I am thankful for it. If you want to keep it real in the streets, get over the awkwardness of the denial and get lost in awe of God.

Chapter 14

The Wall-Mart Test

John 21:7: "Then the disciple whom Jesus loved said to Peter, "It is the Lord!" As soon as Simon Peter heard him say, "It is the Lord," he wrapped his outer garment around him (for he had taken it off) and jumped into the water (NIV)."

As a student, the last day of school was always one of, if not the best day of the year. I have found that as a teacher, that is only sometimes the case. If I am honest, sometimes I was ready to never have a class again. I think back to a first-year biology class. I loved every kid in that room, but the 31 I had that year did not work well together. The nice way to say it is that it was a long year. The funny thing is that class became one of my all-time favorite groups of students. For every class like that, I can remember 5 more times that I was sad when it ended.

At the start of every year, I tell the kids that this class will be like a family. Throughout the year, we will see each other's highs and lows. We will celebrate together and work through some sadness. I found that to be the case when my wife was diagnosed with cancer. The kids that year did not realize it, but they helped me through it daily. Just like a family, we will do life together. Just because we become like family does not mean we will always like each other. Even if the family does not like each other, they are always there for each other. The same is true for all of my classes.

I tell the kid that our relationship will be judged by the Wall-Mart test. While I am unsure if it counts as a scientific test, it's the litmus test I use to see if a former student likes or hates me. Let me explain the parameters of the experiment. It does not have to be a Wal-Mart; it can be any store with long aisles. Let's say you see me coming down the aisle, and you quickly turn and go in the opposite direction. It would be a safe bet to say that you don't like me very much. If you see me coming and start heading towards me, yelling, "Hey, Coach Hall, " it is a safe bet to say that you like being in my class.

That is one of the biggest wins a teacher can experience in their career. Hearing about what is going on in a student's life and seeing the excitement it gives them is incredible. It is not 100% accurate, but I can tell what category students will fall into on the last day of class. I hope that as our time together draws to a close if you see me in the grocery store, you will be excited to tell me how this book helped you walk with Jesus.

Graduation Gift

One fantastic tradition of finishing school to be a part of was sending out graduation invitations. Not only does it let people know of your accomplishments, but most of the time, people would give you a gift in return. Most were cash to help you with whatever you would do next. Sometimes, something minor, like a twenty-dollar bill, may seem insignificant, but it can be significant. A small gift at the time can become a building block for the future. A gift that becomes a building block for the future is one of the best things you could ever give anyone. Don't forget the best gift will always be the gospel.

The good news is that I have a gift for you to make it through this journey with me. I have saved the two biggest takeaways from Peter's story for the last chapter. They are the most significant things to take away as we get over the pains of denial and go out and live for Jesus. In our journey, we have looked at past denial and instructions for the future. The last two points from John chapter 21 deal with our present situation.

139

As we look at the following verses, I want you to examine two things. The first is how personal this conversation is between Jesus and Peter. Other people were there, but Jesus was focused on this moment with Peter. The second is how Jesus's words come from a place of love. Jesus is not shaming Peter with his questions. He is getting his hands on the wound of Peter's actions to heal him.

John 21:15-19: *"15 When they had finished eating, Jesus said to Simon Peter, "Simon son of John, do you love me more than these?" "Yes, Lord," he said, "you know that I love you." Jesus said, "Feed my lambs." 16 Again Jesus said, "Simon son of John, do you love me?" He answered, "Yes, Lord, you know that I love you." Jesus said, "Take care of my sheep." 17 The third time he said to him, "Simon son of John, do you love me?" Peter was hurt because Jesus asked him the third time, "Do you love me?" He said, "Lord, you know all things; you know that I love you." Jesus said, "Feed my sheep. 18 Very truly, I tell you, when you were younger, you dressed yourself and went where you wanted, but when you are old you will stretch out your hands, and someone else will dress you and lead you where you do not want to go." 19 Jesus said this to indicate the kind of death by which Peter would glorify God. Then he said to him, "Follow me! (NIV)"*

Do You Love Me?

Do you love me? While that seems like a straightforward question, it can be more complex. While there are only two answer choices, those choices have a deep meaning. While both answers are short and to the point, the actions of those answers look different. If you answer yes, how you interact with that person will look like 1st Corinthians 13:4-7: *"4 Love is patient, love is kind. It does not envy, it does not boast, it is not proud. 5 It does not dishonor others, it is not self-seeking, it is not easily angered, it keeps no record of wrongs. 6 Love does not delight in evil but rejoices with the truth. 7 It always protects, always trusts, always hopes, always perseveres (NIV)."* We know that, as Christians, our job is to love people as God loves us. 1st Corinthians 13:4-7 is an excellent picture of that love.

If your answer to that question is no, then how you interact with that person will look drastically different from the above description. While saying "yes, I love you" to the question is easy, it is difficult to live that answer out. If you love someone, you can't walk away. I can best explain that using a quote from Captain America and the Winter Soldier. While Steve's best friend Bucky is trying to kill him, Steve looks at him and says, "I am with you till the end of the line." If you stick with someone through the good and the bad until the end, you genuinely love them.

Jesus asks Peter that question three separate times. I believe that God is asking us that right now. Do you love me? It is easy to say yes while loving other things just as much or more than you love God. That's why I love how Jesus asks Peter these questions. The first question added "more than these" to the end. Theologians debate if Jesus meant the fish or the other disciples. I think the point Jesus makes is asking Peter is your love for me above everything else. So, we must ask ourselves the same question. Do we love God more than anything else? That is more difficult to answer, but it is something Jesus spoke about earlier in his ministry. Look at Luke 14:25-26 "*25 Large crowds were traveling with Jesus, and turning to them he said: 26 "If anyone comes to me and does not hate father and mother, wife and children, brothers and sisters—yes, even their own life—such a person cannot be my disciple (NIV).*"

Jesus's point in saying this was to show that following him and your love for him must be the top priority in your life. When you compare your love for something or someone to your love for Jesus, how much you love Jesus should make the love you have for other things look like hate. Does that describe your love for God? I can tell you when I was denying God and living for myself, God was not my top priority or love. Maybe you had days when God was not your first love and priority. Or perhaps you have had a year or years like that. The good news is that our past sins do not take away our hope in the future when our life is in Christ.

Dumbo

The largest elephant ever recorded was an African elephant found in Angola. It weighed 24,000 pounds and stood over 13 feet tall. It would be challenging, if not impossible, to try to hide an elephant half that size in your bedroom. The people you are in a relationship with, either as a family member or spouse, would notice if you were keeping an elephant in your bedroom. It would be moronic to try and act like the elephant does not exist.

My fear is that you may be like me. I can look back on parts of my life where I was not living for God and just kept thinking everything was fine. The problem was that everything was not okay because my actions prevented me from being as close to Jesus as I should have been. While you may not think your denial is as big as an elephant, I can tell you that's how mine felt. I can't know for sure, but I bet that is how Peter felt.

The old saying goes, you must address the elephant in the room. Jesus's conversation with Peter after breakfast does just that. It would be easy to think that Jesus is shaming Peter, but in reality, he is building him up. We know from scripture that Jesus did not come to shame or condemn the world (John 3:17). So, we know if he was not shaming Peter when he addressed the elephant in the room, he is not shaming us when he discusses our elephant. Look at Jesus's response after he answers Jesus' question. Jesus does not bring up the past. He does not tell Peter, "Sure did not look like you loved me when I was arrested." After Peter says he loves him, Jesus gives him a command.

What can we take from this exchange? The first is that Jesus has a purpose for the relationship. After every one of Peter's answers, Jesus tells him to take care of what means the most to him: us. The second is that Jesus has a plan for Peter's life. Even after he denied him, he told him how his life would glorify God all the way to his death. This is what Jesus is trying to show Peter and us. Jesus already knew Peter loved him, but he needed to address the elephant between them and tell Peter to move forward. There is no sin in your life that is not paid for by Jesus. The only thing keeping you from moving forward with Jesus is you.

Another story from scripture that gives us a clue to what it looks like to follow God is the story of Jesus and the rich young man found in Matthew, Mark, and Luke's gospel account. The only thing that kept him from following Jesus was him. He could not give up his life. While you may be ready to follow Jesus, are you prepared to let go of the past and move on? When you are, then the elephant in the room between you and Jesus can turn into Dumbo and can fly away. When the elephant is gone, it creates space to move closer to God. So feed that elephant the truth from Jesus and follow him.

I was one way, and now I am completely different. And what happened in between was him.

The difference between Peter at the Shavuot festival (Pentecost) and him at the Passover festival is dramatically different. Peter said the right things to Jesus on the night of his arrest. The problem was that his actions did not back them up. The consequence of these actions was Peter's heartbreak. I can attest to the fact that heartbreak is the actual result of denying Jesus. It was how I felt the night of my denial, as well as other times I was not living for the Lord.

When we see Peter after this breakfast on the beach with Jesus, he is entirely different. Peter goes from denying Jesus to the ones who put him on trial to proclaiming him as Christ and blaming them for his murder. So, how did Peter go from standing on the sidelines to the middle of the arena? It was not the breakfast or where the conversation took place. The pain of Peter's denial ended when he accepted Jesus's invitation to forgiveness.

Who gives you the invitation to an event is essential. If the guy at the gas station invites you to meet the president of the United States, I probably wouldn't give it too much thought. Why? Because there is a good chance that the invitation was fake. If the vice president of the United States invites you to meet the president, you know it's a real opportunity.

You know Jesus' invitation is real because he was the only one who could give it. Consider what Paul tells us in 2nd Corinthians 5:21:*"God made him who had no sin to be sin for us, so that in him we might become the righteousness of God (NIV)."* Jesus counted the cost and went to the cross to pay our debt. That's why he is the only one who can offer us forgiveness from God. Reconciliation with God is the only real way to change your life. How do you go from denial of Jesus to proclaiming Jesus? By radical encounter with Jesus and accepting his invitation.

3 Foot World

I want to give you our family motto as my last encouragement for our journey. God gave us this and held us together during the bad times. It was also the inspiration for my first book. The phrase is simple: "Stay in your three-foot world." Basically, it's to control what you can and trust God with what you can't.

The last thing Peter asks Jesus about at breakfast on the beach is John. Jesus' response is our final takeaway from John 21. John 21:20-23 *"20 Peter turned and saw that the disciple whom Jesus loved was following them. (This was the one who had leaned back against Jesus at the supper and had said, "Lord, who is going to betray you?") 21 When Peter saw him, he asked, "Lord, what about him?" 22 Jesus answered, "If I want him to remain alive until I return, what is that to you? You must follow me." 23 Because of this, the rumor spread among the believers that this disciple would not die. But Jesus did not say that he would not die; he only said, "If I want him to remain alive until I return, what is that to you (NIV)?"*

Too often, we get caught up in things we can't control or that don't really matter to our plan and purpose from God. That's what Peter did when he asked about John. He starts to focus on things outside of his control. What is in our control is following Jesus. We will always have control over that, no matter our surroundings or circumstances. We can also always be active in his mission of telling the world the gospel story. If we can trust God with our salvation, we can trust him with things outside our control.

Thanks, Coach

Billy Graham once said ""A coach will impact more people in one year than the average person will in an entire lifetime." I know that to be true. I was lucky to work under and learn from some incredible coaches in college. From my start as a manager for the baseball team to my time as a student assistant for basketball and graduate assistant for softball, I was blessed to work for some fantastic people. One thing that stood out from them was how they tried to leave everyone, and everything better than they found it.

I have used the phrase "leave it better than you found it" for years in my coaching career. This did not just apply to locker rooms or dugouts; I also tried to make that happen in all my kids' lives. That was my purpose for writing this book. I pray that everyone walks away from this journey better than we started—not because of anything I wrote, but because they encountered Jesus.

No self-help book will radically change your life the way Jesus can. That can only happen when you encounter the risen Savior. An encounter with Jesus always leaves you better than you were before. Jesus is the ultimate living example of leaving something better than how he found it. If you are skeptical, then let me point you to the evidence. The first thing is that the Bible is full of stories of how people encountered God and were radically changed. The most significant piece of evidence I can show you is my life. I was dead in my sin with no hope, and now I am alive in Christ. Today, you can have that by trusting in Jesus as your Lord and Savior. You can also get over the pains of denial by having a challenging conversation with him about your mistakes and accepting his invitation of grace.

I Love You All, Class Dismissed

To my students,

I can not express how much of a blessing each of you has been to me. You taught me something even in the bad moments or when we disagreed. God was using each of you to help shape me personally. I am better because of each of you. God also used you to shape my ministry.

Remember that we are all weird but fearfully and wonderfully made. Each of you has a God-given talent. Don't waste your life; step into what God has for you. You can find that by spending time with him and drinking deeply from the Bible. As you do that, you will realize you are starting to look more like Jesus. There is no more excellent person to try and emulate.

When in doubt, just be cool, man. Remember that life is short, so don't stress out about it. Part of being cool is being patient. The Navy SEALs have a saying: "Don't run to your death." So, take your time and be where your feet are. Remember, God has you there for a reason.

Make sure you overuse "I love you." Because those small words can change someone's life. The letter at the front of the book can testify to its power. Do it because God is madly in love with you. When you step into that love, it will spill over to all areas of your life. People will see that the love you show them is genuine. Then, you can point them to the source of that love.

Don't lie, cheat, steal, or tolerate anyone who does. It is essential to know who you surround yourself with. Remember Paul's words in 1st Corinthians 15:33: *"Do not be misled: "Bad company corrupts good character (NIV)."* Pick friends and, most importantly, a spouse who loves Jesus more than you do.

Little things make big things happen. If you want to see God move in significant ways in your life, then focus on the little details daily. Make sure you are getting in the word. Find time to pray for yourself and others. If you are unsure what that looks like, remember the words of Jesus in Mark 12:30-31: *"30 Love the Lord your God with all your heart and soul and with all your mind and with all your strength. 31 The second is this: 'Love your neighbor as yourself. There is no commandment greater than these (NIV)."*

Always remember that two is one, and one is none. That's a great rule to ensure you have squared away with what you need. It is also a good rule to never leave the house without Jesus. When we have him, we are never alone. So even when we fail, he won't.

Even if you never physically sat in my classroom, you are one of my kids now. The same thing I tried to instill and show my classes was what I put in this book. So, as you are about to turn the page and walk out of my class, I want to pray for you. There is power in praying scripture. So today, I want to Pray Numbers 6:24-26 over your life *"24 ""The Lord bless you and keep you; 25 the Lord make his face shine on you and be gracious to you; 26 the Lord turn his face toward you and give you peace (NIV).""*

I love you all! Class dismissed.

About
Kharis Publishing:

Kharis Publishing, an imprint of Kharis Media LLC, is a leading Christian and inspirational book publisher based in Aurora, Chicago metropolitan area, Illinois. Kharis' dual mission is to give voice to under-represented writers (including women and first-time authors) and equip orphans in developing countries with literacy tools. That is why, for each book sold, the publisher channels some of the proceeds into providing books and computers for orphanages in developing countries so that these kids may learn to read, dream, and grow. For a limited time, Kharis Publishing is accepting unsolicited queries for nonfiction (Christian, self-help, memoirs, business, health and wellness) from qualified leaders, professionals, pastors, and ministers. Learn more at: https://kharispublishing.com/

www.ingramcontent.com/pod-product-compliance
Lightning Source LLC
LaVergne TN
LVHW022219170125
801528LV00021B/655